PISCES

20 FEBRUARY – 20 MARCH

First published in Great Britain 2012
by Mills & Boon, an imprint of Harlequin (UK) Limited,
Eton House, 18-24 Paradise Road, Richmond, Surrey TW9 1SR

HOROSCOPES 2013 © Dadhichi Toth 2012

ISBN: 978 0 263 90263 1

Typeset by Midland Typesetters

Harlequin (UK) policy is to use papers that are natural, renewable and recyclable products and made from wood grown in sustainable forests. The logging and manufacturing processes conform to the legal environmental regulations of the country of origin.

Printed and bound in Spain
by Blackprint CPI, Barcelona

Dedicated to

The Light of Intuition

Sri V. Krishnaswamy—mentor and friend

With thanks to

Joram and Isaac

Special thanks to

Nyle Cruz for her creative input

and

Janelle Cook for editorial support

⚲ ABOUT DADHICHI ⚲

Dadhichi is one of Australia's foremost astrologers and is frequently seen on TV and in the media. He has the unique ability to draw from complex astrological theory to provide clear, easily understandable advice and insights for people who want to know what their future may hold.

In the 28 years that Dadhichi has been practising astrology, face reading and other esoteric studies, he has conducted over 10,000 consultations. His clients include celebrities, political and diplomatic figures, and media and corporate identities from all over the world.

Dadhichi's unique blend of astrology and face reading helps people fulfil their true potential. His extensive experience practising western astrology is complemented by his research into the theory and practice of eastern forms of astrology.

Dadhichi has been a guest on many Australian television shows and several of his political and worldwide forecasts have proved uncannily accurate. He appears regularly on Australian television networks and is a regular columnist for online and offline Australian publications.

His websites—

www.astrology.com.au and
www.face reader.com

attract hundreds of thousands of visitors each month and offer a wide variety of features, helpful information and services.

MESSAGE FROM
◎ DADHICHI ◎

Hello and welcome to your 2013 horoscope book!

The key to any successful relationship is communication. This is no secret and relates not only to personal one-on-one romantic relationships, but relationships in general. During 2013, the transit of Jupiter through the sign of Gemini highlights the fact that communication is the foundation of happiness and understanding in relationships. If you've been avoiding talking, sharing your feelings or opening up to the one you love, you can't expect your relationship to go very far, can you?

Effective communication is a form of self-education in which you are open to listening to another's point of view, adapting yourself and at some stage changing your habitual psychological patterns to accommodate the person you love. This can also be translated to business relationships, political interactions and any other relationship in which we empathise and feel the other person's needs.

Many of us are so busy trying to change the world that we forget that a better world starts with our own selves, which is why I am highlighting the fact that communication and self-improvement are the starting point for improving the world at large. By avoiding this, we shift responsibility to someone else and ultimately become the victims of our own lives.

The deeper level of relationships has to do with sexual intimacy. Saturn in the sign of Scorpio points to the fact that the coming 12 months will test us in this area of our lives and we need to be conscious that physical intimacy is really only an extension of our psychological and emotional connectedness to others. It doesn't matter which star sign you are born under, these planets will affect all of us in much the same way. Of course, depending on your Sun sign, the way in which you deal with this will change, but make no mistake about it; communication and intimacy are extremely important keywords for this coming period of time.

Fortunately, Jupiter expands our awareness, so this means we are more likely to be open to the possibilities of being ready, willing and able to meet people halfway and truly identify with where they are at. Once this happens, you will start to feel the benefits of true communication. But clear communication is not just about the words that come out of our mouths. It has more to do with feeling the other person's point of view and doing our best to compassionately understand what they are trying to convey.

This year I have made it a point not to focus too much on bigger picture predictions but rather to simplify the message by saying that 'charity begins at home'. In reflecting the true traits of Jupiter, we must endeavour to do our best by helping our nearest and dearest, listening to their needs and largely doing what needs to be done on the home front before we look further afield.

Education isn't so much about degrees, diplomas and other intellectual accomplishments as it is about developing wisdom through a sensitive understanding of the experiences that life brings us. If Jupiter is to be of any use to us during 2013, we need to be receptive to the most personal aspects of our lives and express the lessons through loving, intimate relationships.

I look forward to being of service to you and hope that these forecasts for the coming 12 months will be of special value in helping you shape your destiny.

Your astrologer,

Dadhichi Toth
www.astrology.com.au
dadhichi@astrology.com.au

⊚ CONTENTS ⊚

CONTENTS
CONTINUED

◎ CONTENTS ◎
CONTINUED

PISCES
PROFILE

MEN NEVER PLAN TO BE FAILURES;
THEY SIMPLY FAIL TO PLAN TO BE
SUCCESSFUL.

William Ward

◎ PISCES SNAPSHOT ◎

Key Life Phrase	I Sacrifice
Zodiac Totem	The Fish
Zodiac Symbol	♓
Zodiac Facts	Twelfth sign of the zodiac; mutable, fruitful, feminine and moist
Zodiac Element	Water
Key Characteristics	Loving, sensitive, intuitive, spiritual, idealistic, victimised and moody
Compatible Star Signs	Aries, Taurus, Cancer, Scorpio, Sagittarius, Capricorn and Pisces

Mismatched Signs		Gemini, Leo, Virgo, Libra and Aquarius
Ruling Planets		Jupiter and Neptune
Love Planets		Moon and Mercury
Finance Planets		Mars and Saturn
Speculation Planet		Moon
Career Planets		Sun and Jupiter
Spiritual and Karmic Planets		Moon, Mars and Pluto
Friendship Planets		Saturn
Destiny Planet		Moon
Famous Pisceans	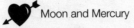	Albert Einstein, Rihanna, Michael Dell, Jean Harlow, Bruce Willis, Kurt Russell, Seal, Jon Bon Jovi, Albert Einstein, Victor Hugo, Aaron Eckhart, Drew Barrymore, Jessica Biel, Eva Mendes, Rachel Weisz, Dakota Fanning and Steve Jobs

Lucky Numbers and Significant Years	2, 3, 9, 11, 12, 18, 20, 21, 27, 29, 30, 36, 38, 45, 47, 48, 54, 56, 57, 74, 75, 81, 83 and 84
Lucky Gems	Yellow sapphire, golden topaz, red coral and pearl
Lucky Fragrances	Rosemary, peppermint, black pepper, bergamot and ylang ylang
Affirmation/ Mantra	I offer my love to you all, but I am grounded
Lucky Days	Monday, Tuesday, Thursday and Sunday

⊚ PISCES OVERVIEW ⊚

The totem of Pisces is the Fish, and just as this creature is immersed in the ocean, so too is the Piscean individual immersed in sea of feelings and idealism. Your feelings run deep and you show your sensitivity on every level of your being. You instinctively want to help others and have often put aside your own interests in order to make life easier for the people you love and care about.

You are a compassionate individual and this is the most notable characteristic of your star sign. You are the person who will pull over to the side of the road to help someone who is in difficulty, or perhaps a creature that is in danger of being run over. Your compassionate nature is in demand by your friends, family and co-workers. If they are in any distress, your presence alone will make them feel calm and reassured.

You like to avoid hard decisions, especially if you know someone is going to get a poor deal. When it comes to close friends and family, you'll do almost anything to help them, but you need to be careful that you don't finish up as the victim. Some Pisceans repeat the victim cycle again and again and can't get themselves out of the rut.

You may surprise others with your intuition and accurate foresight despite being seen as a dreamer.

Dreamy Pisces

You don't always approach life in the most rational or easily understood manner. In fact, you may seem like a bit of a daydreamer, thinking about all sorts of things others wouldn't give a minute's thought to, but that is part of your charm.

If you have the inclination, you can become a great psychic, clairvoyant or medium due to this inbuilt power. However, intuition only goes so far, and in order to develop this intuition, you need to expand your thinking processes—difficult as it may be at times. This will create more balance in your life.

You have an innate understanding of the connectedness of life, and others would consider you to be spiritual, even though religion, in the strictest sense of the word, is not really your forté. You have strong visions of the way you'd like to see the world, but this doesn't always fit the picture of reality as you experience it.

There's a gap between where you fit in the world and where you'd like to be, which is why you may find yourself a little out of step with what's happening around you. You take in both good and bad vibrations from those around you, which is why you must learn to be a little less sensitive so that the moods and circumstances of those in your immediate environment don't drag you down.

You are a sentimental individual and friends and family may see you shed a tear or two while watching a movie that is emotionally moving. You are gentle, impressionable and also receptive, and want to share your feelings, but you're equally happy to share the feelings of others, even if those feelings are tinged with suffering. This is your way of communicating love.

Using your mystical creative talents to uplift your community and the world at large will help you find meaning in your life. If, however, you don't manage to reconcile these two opposing views of the world, you could become too reliant on alcohol, drugs or other addictive patterns of living that can undermine your long-term happiness.

⊚ PISCES CUSPS ⊚

ARE YOU A CUSP BABY?

Being born on the crossover of two star signs means that you have the qualities of both. Sometimes you don't know whether you're Arthur or Martha! Some of my clients can't quite figure out whether they are indeed their own star sign or the one before or after. This is to be expected because being born on the borderline means you take on aspects of both. The following will give you an overview of the subtle effects of these cusp dates and how they affect your personality.

Pisces–Aquarius Cusp

If you were born between the 20th and the 26th of February, you were born under the cusp of Aquarius and Pisces. This means that you are influenced by some of the elements and personality traits of Aquarius.

Pisces is a water sign and Aquarius is air, so you sometimes find it difficult to balance the emotional and intellectual sides of your nature. You find decision-making more difficult than the 'typical' Piscean as you have this extra influence. Pisceans generally run with their intuition or gut feeling. But throw into the mix the thinking of an Aquarian, and you have a 'heart versus head' and 'head versus heart' battle. It can be quite confusing and you may find it a bit much at times.

Pisceans are daydreamers, so it is a bonus that the intellectual and communicative aspects of Aquarius are within you. This will endow you with a much more down-to-earth approach to life and love. Being born on this cusp will also give you the ability to take traditional concepts and turn them into ideas that are useful in assisting others, either as individuals or a group. Humanitarian work attracts you, Pisces, and you may find your niche in organisations or hospitals that give you the opportunity to communicate so much of this Pisces–Aquarius combination.

INTUITIVE HEALER

You are also an intuitive healer and can alleviate the suffering of friends, family and people in general. You have a wonderful destiny and will be sought after as a truly unconditional lover and friend.

It is a blessing to be born under this cusp and it gives you a destiny that is unique. You really enjoy helping others less fortunate, whether it is on a local or global scale, and this quality will endear you to those near and far.

Pisces–Aries Cusp

If you are born between the 14th and the 20th of March, you exhibit some of the fiery energies of the next zodiac sign, Aries. You are an intense Piscean who can be a little possessive and demanding when it comes to love. Other

Pisceans can handle this type of dominant personality, but you will need some give and take from Aries.

TUG OF WAR

Trying to balance the elements of fire and water will be a challenge for you, Pisces. The quiet and indecisive Pisces may get pushed around a little by the fire of Aries, which can make you aggressive in your approach.

Your primary concern in life is helping others and giving help freely when it is needed most. Your nature is creative and enterprising and you want to achieve something in this world. The strong ego of Aries will make it hard for you to keep yourself and others in balance, and there will be times when you feel like a pendulum, swinging between egotism and selflessness. This may become a lifelong challenge that will force you to make compromises in your life.

The influence of Aries also brings with it an intensity that could make you physically sick if you are unable to balance your ambitions and emotions. If you can get this element of your personality under control and strike a happy medium, you have a great chance of achieving success and living a fulfilling life.

◉ PISCES CELEBRITIES ◉

FAMOUS MALE:
STEVE JOBS

Steve Jobs was born on the 24th of February, 1955. As a Pisces with an Aquarian cast, he had a radical and innovative mind, and the ability to create unique inventions.

A native of Pisces is often regarded as a dreamer, or as someone with their head in the clouds, but Steve Jobs was not one of them. Instead, he represented the highest calibre of Piscean individuals who dream big dreams and who, through impeccable timing and hard work, make those dreams a reality.

If you look at the impact that Steve has had on technology in no less than six industries—personal computers, film, animation, music, telephones and digital publishing—you will realise the impact that this man has had over the past 30 years.

But Steve Jobs' life and career was never a walk in the park. Like most successful people, he went through incredible ups and downs. And although at first glance his triumphs don't fall into typical Piscean territory, there is still a great deal of spiritual and humanitarian benefit that has come through his inventions and contributions.

The typical Piscean is restless by nature, and, if the task is boring, their focus may not be very good. We can see this in Steve's early development when he dropped out of Reed College in Portland, Oregon after only one semester. And when he did go to college, he would only attend classes that covered topics he was interested in. After dropping out, he decided to work with video game manufacturer Atari. Through this job he raised enough money to go to India and during this time he became an avowed Buddhist. This shows his spiritual inclinations, which is typical with Pisceans.

In 1976, he and Steve Wozniak developed the first prototype of the Apple computer. Over the next two decades he helped in the development of the iMac, iTunes, iPod, iPhone and iPad. With its almost obsessive commitment to design and user-friendliness, Apple has quickly become one of the world's most-loved brands. Steve Jobs died in October 2011, but with this incredible legacy, he continues to shape the future of digital media.

FAMOUS FEMALE:
RIHANNA

Rihanna was born on the 20th of February, 1988, which makes her a Piscean born on the cusp of Aquarius. Endowed with the idealism of Pisces, she also has the forward-thinking, revolutionary spirit of Aquarius. This makes Rihanna a woman who aspires to reach for the stars and use her creative abilities to change the world and do something of lasting worth.

Those born under Pisces have a dreamy quality about them. This intangible aspect is what we call 'star quality', and it has helped Rhianna skyrocket to fame. In fact, she has obtained eleven number one pop singles on the *Billboard* Hot 100 chart, and sold over 25 million albums. Her fifth album, *Loud*, sold 2.8 million copies worldwide in just three months.

In true Piscean form, she is never averse to using her power, influence and talents to help a good cause. Pisceans always feel a sense of spiritual connectedness to those who are less fortunate than themselves. Recently, she assisted in a charity gala event to help the victims of Hurricane

Katrina, and in 2006 she created The Believe Foundation for terminally ill children. This also reminds us of other world-famous Piscean stars, such as Elizabeth Taylor, who also worked tirelessly for charitable causes.

PISCES

AT LARGE

SUCCESS IS HOW HIGH YOU
BOUNCE WHEN YOU HIT BOTTOM.

George S. Patton

◎ PISCES MAN ◎

PISCES MAN: SNAPSHOT

Evolved

Emotional

Social

Psychic

Idealistic

Adaptable

According to astrology, the signs of the zodiac represent the evolutionary stages of an individual, commencing with Aries and finishing with Pisces. Astrologers believe that Pisces is the most spiritually advanced of the signs. Their motivation in life is to give, serve and love, and this infuses most of their actions.

At some point in your life, Pisces, spiritual interests and personal development will occupy a large part of your mind. Yours is the final sign of human evolution in the astrological scheme. It should come as no surprise that you'll aspire to knowledge that is beyond this world, and as you grow older and mature, your psychic powers will develop. As a result, you will be seen as a source of valuable wisdom to all around you.

As a male born under Pisces, you are more than capable of fully expressing the feminine aspects of your character. This doesn't mean you're not masculine, but you seem to engender the New Age model of what people refer to as the perfect blend of male and female energies.

Generally, you prefer to be with positive and upbeat people. If you are exposed to negativity, it is very likely to cause mood swings due to your absorptive personality. This is likely to be the case in the early part of your life when you're not quite capable of bringing all of these emotional crosscurrents under control.

Pisces is an emotional sign, and although you give a lot, you also need to be nurtured and loved. Try to surround yourself with people who have something to give and who are not always taking from you. Like a sponge, you tend to absorb negativity around you and this will ultimately cause you poor health and disappointment in your relationships.

You have an idealistic view of the world, but the reality is not in keeping with what you believe life should be. Try to accept the world and the people in it as they are. You must learn to be more secure in yourself to bring satisfaction into your life. Those who are fortunate enough to be part of your life should learn to treat you with sensitivity and love. In fact, you deserve the same as what you give, so never be afraid of demanding a fair deal, whether it's on a personal or professional level.

Friends regard you as an oasis in the desert of life, and when troubles befall them, they know they can rely on you. Even if you're not able to help them solve the problem, you're never too busy to make yourself available to console them in their time of need.

You are an extremely sensitive individual, and when it comes to making decisions, your conclusions often settle around whether you are going to hurt others in the process. This is one of your key lessons in life, and you must balance the needs of others with your own so that you don't become a victim of your compassionate nature.

When you are among friends and colleagues, you may seem like a bit of a dreamer, or perhaps self-absorbed and 'zoned out'. This can be mistaken for a lack of interest on your part, but you are actually in some creative space that needs your attention. This is a form of meditation in action, and it is part and parcel of who you are. You might try to explain this to others, but many will not understand where you're coming from.

Your view of the world can be idealistic, and unscrupulous people will see you as an easy target. They will spin a

Creative Pisces

Your creative side can come up with some amazing work and unusual ideas. If you're involved in this type of vocation, you will certainly stand out from the crowd. You can tap into human nature on a level that is only accessible to few, and you can come up with some great ideas.

hard luck story, which you will probably believe, and take advantage of your kindness and compassion. If this happens to you often, it may cause you to lose money and dent your pride.

In business, being honest in your dealings may work against you if you don't guard against being too soft and believing everything you are told. You must learn to draw some boundaries before actively engaging in a business deal with others, even if they start out as a friend. Just remember, business is business.

Women are attracted to you because you're sensitive to their needs and provide them with the caring and compassionate support that they require. As a result, you'll make an excellent husband, father and homemaker.

⊚ PISCES WOMAN ⊚

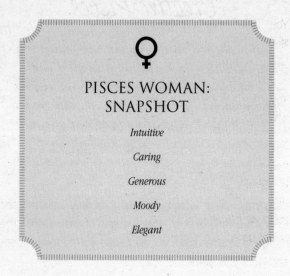

PISCES WOMAN: SNAPSHOT

Intuitive

Caring

Generous

Moody

Elegant

The Piscean woman is the epitome of elegance. You have a depth and grace that is not easily matched by females of any other star sign. Words are not necessary for a Piscean woman as her demeanour, presence or a casual glance all express her personality in a most notable way. The Piscean woman is sensual and mystical and brings forth the ideals that women everywhere aspire to.

As you know, Neptune, your spiritual planet, rules over the deep blue ocean, and Piscean women can be just as deep and mysterious. Pisces is a feminine sign and you symbolise feminine qualities perfectly. You have an aura that draws people to you and they immediately sense your transparent and caring nature.

You look beneath the surface of things and live your life in a more unconventional manner than your peers. Human nature fascinates you, so you prefer to surround yourself with those who also have some depth of vision. You do not get along well with superficial people as you see them as being without substance.

You have an extraordinary imagination and wish to express that in every part of your life. You may find it puzzling that others are a little slow to grasp your ideas, and you could be confused about why these ideas are seen as impractical by some. It is just that your vision might be considered years ahead of its time.

Money is not your primary motivation, but that doesn't mean you're not interested in it. To you, money is a form of energy, a measure of your own activity and love, and it's used to help others and possibly even uplift humanity in some way. You're quick to grasp an opportunity to be of assistance, even with mundane tasks. Piscean women are extremely sociable and artistic, and the idea of combining creativity and fun appeals to you. You have a strong love of nature and easily connect with the beauty around you. You have a tremendous respect for the magnificence of life and its expression in art, music and any other artistic pursuit. Cultural activities capture your attention and imagination, and you'll need to surround yourself with likeminded people. If that's not possible, you'll be quite happy to spend time alone and investigate the mysteries of the Universe on your own.

You find it hard to be involved in any form of confrontation, and when you find yourself dealing with antagonistic or aggressive individuals, you tend to shut down. In this sort of situation, you prefer to suffer quietly rather than deal with the problem at hand. Sacrifice doesn't necessarily mean you have to totally surrender, but, at times, your emotional life can become too overwhelming. This is something that you will have to learn to deal with sooner or later.

STAY POSITIVE

Piscean women need to stay away from alcohol as there is a tendency to acquire addictions. Keep active and don't let negative thoughts or self-defeating behaviour drag you down.

Generally, your philosophy is to make peace, not war, and this is probably one of your most charming character traits. If you take a more proactive approach to life and implement your visions in meaningful work, you'll easily fulfil your inner dreams. As well as that, it will give you the opportunity to do what you do best—uplift the lives of those you come into contact with.

☉ PISCES CHILD ☉

Piscean children are born into the final stage of human evolution, which makes them old souls. You probably already know that they have a rather mature attitude to things, even from their earliest childhood. The Piscean baby is caring, loving and sensitive in nature. The warmth and love they possess is easily reflected in their eyes, and this is one of their most attractive features.

As your Piscean child grows older, you will find them teaching you things and offering lessons about life that will amaze you. You will wonder where these gems of wisdom have come from, but this all part of the spiritual legacy they bring from their previous lives.

They also bring a breadth of knowledge and human understanding that people five times their age may not have developed. Even if they don't speak, they can express their unique insights and knowledge through a gesture or even a casual glance.

Your child will be extremely artistic and can express themselves musically or artistically. Their teachers may comment that they're a 'natural' with art, music or drama. Piscean children are always eager to share, and, where possible, you should get involved in activities with them. Just being around your Pisces child can be very uplifting, and it will draw out your own loving and compassionate nature.

A Piscean baby can be dreamy and sometimes a bit distracted, so they need a good routine of discipline to keep them grounded. But don't be too harsh with rules, regulations and timetable; punishing them can leave deep wounds in their psyche. Discipline should be gentle but sufficient to understand the rules of life. If you can strike a balance between discipline and play, you will have a well developed Piscean child.

WATER LOVERS

As Pisces is a water sign, there's no doubt your child will want to be involved in all types of water sports. Swimming, fishing and other games in or near the water will be wonderful activities to balance their minds and strengthen their bodies.

Piscean children are always happy to share, and they will give up their possessions and resources to friends. By teaching them the value of sharing, you bring out an even greater part of their personality. While doing this, instil in them that they don't need to be taken advantage of or become the victim of bullying, and that they don't have to keep giving just because it's in their nature.

A pet will do wonders for your Piscean child and help foster their caring and sharing nature. They will take great pleasure in nurturing their small pet, and they will treat them like their best friend. This will help set the stage for their later development as a caring member of the community. All in all, it's hard to beat the heartfelt love you'll get from a child born under the sign of Pisces.

PISCES LOVER

Those born under the zodiac sign of Pisces are rather fragile and susceptible in love. This is because you give yourself easily, fully and unconditionally, and are not aware of flaws in your partner. You are unreserved and non-judgmental in your love, but once hurt you will find it difficult to recover in the short term, and may even doubt your well-developed intuition.

You don't really study those you are attracted to or fall in love with because you are inclined to be a bit of a dreamer. You are always dreaming of love and perfection, but you need to exercise some caution if you are going to have a fulfilling relationship. Your idea of a perfect love is not really in keeping with reality, and this can cause you disappointments along the way.

In your younger years, you may feel that you will never find someone who will fulfil you, but you will be persistent, keeping your desires realistic. Once you feel you have met the person of your dreams, you will give yourself completely and utterly.

You need a lot of love and acceptance, and a partner who is going to stimulate your mind on a day-to-day basis. You are protective of your partner, and even if they don't return your unconditional love, you're still prepared to give yourself wholeheartedly in the hope that they, too, may enjoy the gift of sharing. But keep your expectations realistic and don't become too needy, or your partner may lose respect for you. Sexually, you must have a partner who can give in return for your wholehearted commitment.

You never allow romance to die, which is the Piscean way. You're continually devising new ways to keep the flames of your passion burning, even into old age. You like to surprise your lover with shows of affection and novel techniques to demonstrate how you feel about them. Candlelit dinners, quiet moments in a natural setting, and even little love notes will let them know your love is true and forever. If your partner starts to feel a little smothered—and you will know this straightaway—it would be wise to cool down for a while and take the pressure off the relationship. You have strong intuitive powers and know precisely how your lover feels, which puts you a step ahead of them. You also sense when and what their problems are, so that you always have a ready-made solution at hand.

KEEPING THE DREAM ALIVE

You don't believe that love is an impossible dream and will work hard to find the right partner. Water signs such as Pisces know how to nurture their partners, and they will pull out all the stops to keep the fires of love alive and burning brightly.

You're so deeply committed to the idea of a long-term and stable relationship that you pursue your love diligently and keep trying to find perfect ways to satisfy your lover. In some ways, Pisces, you could be coined the perfect lover because you truly wish to make your dreams a reality.

Sex and intimacy are very important to Pisces. The physical expression of love is an extension of who you are, and you're no less giving in these matters than you are in love. Venus and Libra dominate the zone of your sexuality, which means that Pisces has a natural affinity for sex and physical intimacy. Once you meet the right person, you can totally surrender yourself and truly understand the joys of lovemaking.

⊙ PISCES FRIEND ⊙

Loyalty and understanding are two of your most endearing qualities as a friend, Pisces. People want to be your friend, and once you make a friend, you will want to keep them for a very long time. This is a sign of your deep and caring nature. What you aim for is quality and not quantity. Each friend is special to you in their own way and you are sensitive to all their idiosyncrasies.

However, as you become emotionally attached to your friends, you need to protect yourself from being taken advantage of. You need to stand up for yourself and not be a victim. There will always be those who see you as easy pickings because of your kind and compassionate ways, so there will be disappointments along the road of life.

You like nothing better than to have a good laugh and catch up with friends. Being a great listener, you are quite happy to hear the problems of others and often try to help them with a solution. This is what friendship means to you.

You are just as happy being alone as you are being at the centre of family get-togethers or office parties. These two sides of your nature may seem at odds with each other, but if you explain it to your friends, it will end their confusion.

You will be drawn to creative and imaginative activities, and the people you meet there will innately understand where you're coming from. You like to do things that are interesting, offbeat and that generate creative impulses, not just in you but in your friends as well. In fact, you like to see your friends excel emotionally, artistically and spiritually.

You pay attention to what makes your friends feel good and go out of your way to create an environment that will make everyone feel great. You radiate a spirit of love in the highest sense, and people will be drawn to you.

You are a complex personality, Pisces, with a sensitivity and depth of emotion that can quickly change from positive to dark if your emotions get the better of you. You'll make many friends due to your genuine attitude and self-sacrificing ways, and you will do anything for those who mean the most to you—and friends are certainly on that list.

◎ PISCES ENEMY ◎

Pisces is an emotional star sign, and once your feelings are hurt, you won't easily forget it. Sometimes, however, you may be the one at fault, and if your ego gets the better of you, it will make the situation worse. When you are in the wrong, you need to admit it—and the sooner the better.

Pisceans, although forgiving, do find it hard to accept an apology. If your faults are pointed out—and you do have some, Pisces—you'd prefer to ignore this information and pretend that nothing happened. However, you can avoid enemies if you can accept constructive criticism and come to grips with the idea that you aren't faultless.

You also need to learn some diplomacy in dealing with friends and workplace associates so that relationships don't deteriorate further. You must never be impulsive without giving due consideration to the issues at hand. You rely on your intuition, which is mostly correct, but there are occasions when you can be mistaken. Keep your ego in check and be aware of your negative thought patterns. They can alter your thinking about a subject and lead you down a path of depression.

PISCES

AT HOME

THERE ARE TWO MISTAKES ONE CAN
MAKE ALONG THE ROAD TO TRUTH:
NOT GOING ALL THE WAY, AND NOT
STARTING.

Buddha

◎ HOME FRONT ◎

Your home, Pisces, will express your desire to live in a fantasy world. You are creative, have a wonderful imagination, and can make your home as fantastic as you want. Living freely in your own space and expressing yourself whenever and however you like pleases you immensely. You are not terribly good at routine and sometimes your home environment deteriorates into a bit of a mess, but this doesn't worry you in the least.

You are a bit of a daydreamer and there is always tomorrow, isn't there, Pisces? Your home is often central to your social life as you love to have friends and family around. Entertaining enables you to share your feelings and love, mostly through your attention to detail and the ambience you create. Atmosphere is very important to you, and scented candles, lighting, table settings, flowers and general atmosphere are all important.

As your totem is two fish going in different directions, you too can find yourself torn between being with others and being alone. You are happy in either situation, but when you are tired of the social scene, you are quite happy to go somewhere quiet and be alone with your thoughts. This is how you recharge your batteries and have 'me' time—something that you don't do often enough because you are always giving to others.

Mood lighting, candles and mirrors will all add to the ambience of your home and reflect your desire to live in a fantasy world. You are a sentimental star sign, Pisces, which is why you like to have photos and mementos of friends and family on display. Your creative side will look for frames that are unusual and add to the fantasy side of your personality. You will also enjoy having flowers around you that stimulate the senses. These can range from the fairly ordinary to the extremely exotic.

As Pisces is a spiritual and artistic sign, your furnishings and accessories might be sourced from the Third World, and this will also satisfy your desire to help those less fortunate than yourself. Statues of Indian gods and goddesses, bright cushions, incense and music will also enhance your home and be a true reflection of you. Your home is also likely to have the energy of a temple-like environment.

You enjoy sharing your home with others and want them to feel comfortable. Your spirituality will shine through and make your dwelling a place where friends want to be. The totem for Pisces is the Fish, so why not have an exotic fish tank or outdoor garden pond as a feature. Not only will it look beautiful, but it will also calm your senses.

KARMA, LUCK AND
◉ MEDITATION ◉

You are an emotional star sign, Pisces, and it is imperative that you spend some time each day in a calm environment to allow yourself to meditate on higher ideals. This will enable you to deal with what the day throws at you, and keep you grounded when the demands of daily life become overwhelming. If you can do this, you will be able to achieve a perfect balance between the world of the spirit and everyday responsibilities.

'I sacrifice' is your personal life phrase as you are always trying to help someone in need. This, however, does not mean that you should sacrifice yourself and become a victim—far from it. The sub-title to your life phrase should be 'I discriminate' so that you are not used as a doormat for people to wipe their feet on.

You have a well-developed intuition, and meditation will help you to deepen this feeling. You are not a person who goes along with a religion or philosophy without thorough research or the conviction that it is what you believe. You need to know that it has relevance and purpose in your life.

Venus is the ruling planet of your past karma and good fortune, and you are lucky in relation to others as you use your charm and feminine energy to help steer you in the right spiritual direction.

Cancer and the Moon rule your future karma, which indicates that your future is tied up with your emotional and spiritual life. This regulates feelings and intuitive responses and also shows that good karma will come to you as a result of your lifelong quest to help others.

Lucky Days

Your luckiest days are Monday, Tuesday, Thursday and Sunday.

Lucky Numbers

Lucky numbers for Pisces include the following. You may wish to experiment with these in lotteries and other games of chance:

9, 18, 27, 36, 45, 54, 63

2, 11, 20, 29, 38, 47, 56

7, 16, 25, 34, 43, 52, 61

Destiny Years

The most significant years in your life are likely to be 2, 3, 9, 11, 12, 18, 20, 21, 27, 29, 30, 36, 38, 45, 47, 48, 54, 56, 57, 74, 75, 81, 83 and 84.

HEALTH, WELLBEING
◉ AND DIET ◉

Water is the predominant element of Pisces, and this will have a very important bearing on your emotions and relationships. Your mental and physical health will be very much connected to how you feel. You are like a sponge in the way you absorb the negativity of others, and this can undermine your health. Learning the art of relaxation will help you remove any self-defeating thought patterns.

You need a regular routine of work and play, adequate exercise and sleep to maintain optimum vitality. Hatha yoga, aerobic exercises and daily stretching are ideal for your star sign and creating a balance in your life. Supple muscles and improved circulation will also help calm and stabilise your emotions.

Your feet, toes and toenails are ruled by the sign of Pisces, so these areas are likely to be constitutionally weak. Internally, your lymphatic system and astral circulatory system, known as the nadis (through which your life force passes), are also under the jurisdiction of Pisces.

When exercising, make sure your shoes fit properly as you want to make fat burning a pleasurable experience that won't deter you from continuing with your program.

The inclusion of Vitamin B complex, beans and legumes will help your circulation and reduce problems in these areas. Ginger in your meals is also a great adjunct to your diet.

Pisceans tend to put on weight easily, and as Jupiter rules the fat tissue in the body, you should reduce your fat intake as this can cause problems for your liver. It can also put extra strain on your feet and legs and hamper your ability to exercise.

Emotional problems can cause you to overeat as a way of compensation. Vitamins A, B and magnesium are important components and supplements for your health. Lots of fruit and vegetables are important, such as broccoli, celery, green peppers, tomatoes and cherries. Soy bean products, eggs and sunflower seeds are also excellent additions to your diet.

❀ FINANCE FINESSE ❀

Pisces individuals are not overly preoccupied with making money, but when they put their minds to it, they can indeed acquire a small fortune. The planet Mars dominates the second zone of Pisces, which governs the moneymaking sphere of your life. Once you decide to earn money, you can do it with great energy and creativity.

At the same time, take care with money as Mars shows that you have a tendency to be impulsive in the way that you spend it. Being an argumentative planet, it also indicates that there will be times throughout your life when money will become a sticking point in your relationships. It is always a good idea to discuss financial matters and come to some agreement before moving forward with someone. This will help you avoid any sorts of problems in finance.

It's interesting to note that Capricorn, which is a rather conservative and thrifty sign, rules your business profitability. When you put your mind to it and pull your head out of the clouds, you can make excellent headway in the financial sphere.

PISCES
AT WORK

CONSIDER HOW HARD IT IS TO
CHANGE YOURSELF AND YOU'LL
UNDERSTAND WHAT LITTLE CHANCE
YOU HAVE IN TRYING TO CHANGE
OTHERS.

Jacob M. Braude

◎ PISCES CAREER ◎

IDEAL PROFESSIONS

Spiritualist/Psychic

Doctor or Nurse

Actor or Artist

Charity worker

Photographer

Social worker

Designer

Sailor

Poet

You may experience difficulties in deciding what type of career you want, Pisces. Piscean-born individuals are quite emotional, so you need to be doing work that gives you satisfaction on an emotional level. As a result, you will need to put some time into researching all the possibilities that may suit you.

You have a caring nature that needs to be expressed in whatever career you choose, so working in the medical field as a doctor or nurse may fulfil this part of your personality.

The Sun and Leo give you a lot of energy and drive in the workplace. The Sun is your willpower and drive, and it is associated with the sixth zone of selfless service.

You have a sense of fair play in the way you work, and this is something that will endear you to your colleagues. You work hard and don't believe that you have a right to anything, but you are responsible for the good when it comes to you—and it will, Pisces.

CREATIVE AND INTUITIVE

Your creative side could be utilised by being an actor, poet or designer. With your well-developed intuition, studies in spiritualism or becoming a psychic may also interest you. Whatever you do, your honesty and integrity will be powerful accessories to the other skills you bring to your work.

Sagittarius rules your career sector, which gives you a love of variety, travel and learning. Your ruling planet, Neptune, could give you an interest in television, film, photography, art, music, dance and other creative areas. You may also be attracted to the helping and healing professions, such as social and welfare work, dietetics or nursing. Your sincere desire to help could lead you to work with children, particularly those with mental or physical disabilities. Pisceans are excellent teachers and education could be another area worth investigating.

☉ PISCES BOSS ☉

If your boss happens to be a Piscean, you will find them quite approachable, considerate, understanding and fair in all their dealings. Although they prefer to be alone rather than dealing with too many people, they will listen to you and try to help solve whatever issues you are may have in the workplace.

You can be reassured that they will be honest in their dealings with you and won't knowingly take advantage of you or your colleagues. They will always take the time to get to the bottom of any problems within the workplace, and they know that a happy and fulfilled employee is of great benefit to the company.

As Pisces is a water sign, your employer could be rather moody and temperamental at times, and you might not know what lies on the other side of the door as you arrive at work. This is a day-to-day thing with Pisces, so you just have to go with the flow and make the best of each day. You might have to work on your intuition to guess what their mood will be.

Pisceans are somewhat creative and unconventional, and working for them can be an adventure in itself. You mustn't be afraid of sharing your opinions as they will appreciate your attention. At times you may see them getting a bit distracted or going off course, so a little guidance for them will not go astray, even if they are the boss.

EMPLOYEES COME FIRST

A Piscean boss will concentrate on the welfare of their employees more than the financial side of the business. While money is needed to run a successful enterprise, a Pisces boss will not automatically have his or her eye on the bottom line.

A Piscean boss is not good at working under pressure, so making decisions with far-reaching consequences will make things hard for them. Anxiety often sets in, and their fertile imagination may get the better of them, making them worry even more.

If you have a Piscean boss, you can encourage them and let them know that you're as loyal to them as they are to you. And if you can be a sounding board for them, they will value you all the more.

◎ PISCES EMPLOYEE ◎

A Piscean employee has a lot of good qualities, but they do require a degree of delicate handling. To bring out the best in them, you need to support them by allowing them to express their imagination in their job. If this is not possible, you will soon have a rather depressed, lazy and apathetic individual on your payroll. This is not a great situation for either of you.

You would be mistaken if you think that money is the primary motivator for a Pisces employee. It is not that they don't need money; it is just that it is not at the top of their priority list. They need freedom to be comfortable at work, but you may have to put some boundaries and direction in place or they could become rather scattered in their approach and daily duties. They need a firm but guiding hand to keep them on track and help them regain any lost interest in their work.

Your Pisces employee needs to enjoy the work they do and use their creativity as much as possible. If their job involves serving others, rendering assistance or giving advice, then rest assured they will do a brilliant job and feel rewarded at the same time. A sense of belonging, an appreciation for what they do and the opportunity to help others takes pride of place in their mind.

Pisces employees conduct themselves well in a business setting. They are loyal, hard working and friendly to their co-workers. They may even surprise you at times with their shrewdness in business, even though they might not appear ambitious. They just quietly work away, biding their time, but they are quite capable of heading up large organisations once they have served enough time to prepare them for a leading role.

Your Pisces employee may be distracted in the workplace due to personal pressures, so if you see that they are detached and antisocial, you can be almost sure there is something wrong in their private life. There is nothing worse than having a Piscean employee who is weighed down by emotional problems as this will drastically affect their performance on the job.

Your Pisces employee is a good mixer in the office, and if they exhibit preoccupation, it would be wise to take them aside and counsel them gently to find out what is wrong. They will appreciate that you have taken the time to notice that all is not wonderful in their personal life, and you will have an employee who will put in that extra ten per cent when required.

PROFESSIONAL RELATIONSHIPS: BEST AND WORST

BEST PAIRING:
PISCES AND CAPRICORN

Count yourself fortunate if you have a Capricorn financial partner, Pisces. Capricorn falls in the zone of financial profitability, which is also considered a zone of friendship, so you win on two fronts—professional and personal.

You are quite idealistic, Pisces, and Capricorn is concrete and practical in the most unambiguous terms. Capricorns are goal-orientated and like anything that can be proved, which is why finance and numbers are the perfect world for them. They also have a great love of security, so building a successful business really works for them.

Capricorns also have a capacity for sustained work and self-sacrifice, with material benefit in mind. You are a selfless worker as well, but you do so for the benefit of others rather than yourself, which is why it would be wise to leave Capricorn in charge of the money coming in and out as they have more self-control than you in this area, Pisces.

The elements of water and earth function quite well together, and although your governing planets are not especially friendly, the opposing forces of your ruling planets can assist in inspiring each other. They will also equalise your energies and bring steadiness to the business relationship.

Capricorn-born individuals like to do well in business, and with their frugality, carefulness and focused approach, they will achieve good results in whatever business they take on. They will not cause you any concern if they are in charge of the financial side of the partnership. In fact, they will be quite happy to let you be in charge of the creative side while they number-crunch to their heart's content. You will have mutual respect for each other, and this is part of why you are an excellent professional match.

Your Capricorn partner will leave you to sort out your emotions and black moods. However, if there is even a whiff of this affecting the smooth running of the business, you will be advised of their displeasure in no uncertain terms.

Your Capricorn partner will earn your respect by being able to sniff out a good deal and teaching you how to become a better business person. They will also teach you how to develop your skill base professionally.

Capricorns can become a bit bogged down in work and life, and this is where you can counterbalance their rather sombre and flat moments. You can do this by showing them that life is not all about money and materialism, and that there are better ways to spend your time than hunched over the computer doing the numbers. Overall, this should be a prosperous business partnership that fulfils you both.

WORST PAIRING:
PISCES AND VIRGO

If you're thinking about getting into a professional relationship with a Virgo, don't even go there! Virgo is dominated by its ruling planet, Mercury, which is completely preoccupied with analysis, attention to detail and practical issues surrounding your commercial relationship. They are also over the top when it comes to criticism, and who needs that twenty-four hours a day?

The earth element of Virgo will keep things on an even keel, but you will feel as though you have no room to express your creative side and imagination. You have the spiritual planets of Jupiter and Neptune governing your life and activities, and these planets are enemies of Mercury.

Your attitude, Pisces, is spontaneous, and you like to do things from the heart, relying on your intuition to keep things on track. You are more inclined to follow your heart than your head, and even if you are not 100 per cent convinced that the situation is what your intuition tells you, you will persist until a solution is reached. This is definitely not the way Virgo works. They will drive you absolutely nuts as they turn over every little pebble—questioning, reasoning and assessing all the details. This will come across as criticism of how you conduct business.

IMPOSSIBLE STANDARDS

You will become impatient with the Virgo desire for perfection, and although you too like things done properly, your benchmark is nowhere near Virgo's.

You are not especially motivated by money, but Virgo has a strong sense of the economies of running a business. To avoid constant arguments over money matters, you may have to turn over full control to Virgo just to get them off your back. All in all, I can safely say that a business venture with Virgo will be more work and frustration than it is really worth.

PISCES
IN LOVE

THERE IS NEVER A TIME OR PLACE
FOR TRUE LOVE. IT HAPPENS
ACCIDENTALLY, IN A HEARTBEAT, IN
A SINGLE FLASHING, THROBBING
MOMENT.

Sarah Dessen

ROMANTIC
◎ COMPATIBILITY ◎

How compatible are you with your current partner, lover or friend? Did you know that astrology can reveal a whole new level of understanding between people simply by looking at their star sign and that of their partner? In this chapter I'd like to share with you some special insights that will help you better appreciate the strengths and challenges using Sun sign compatibility.

The Sun reflects your drive, willpower and personality. The essential qualities of two star signs blend like two pure colours producing an entirely new colour. Relationships, similarly, produce their own emotional colours when two people interact. The following is a general guide to your romantic prospects with others and how by knowing the astrological 'colour' of each other, the art of love can help you create a masterpiece.

When reading the following I ask you to remember that no two star signs are ever totally incompatible. With effort and compromise, even the most 'difficult' astrological matches can work. Don't close your mind to the full range of life's possibilities! Learning about each other and ourselves is the most important facet of astrology.

Each star sign combination is followed by the elements of those star signs and the result of their combining: for instance, Aries is a fire sign and Aquarius is an air sign and this combination produces a lot of 'hot air'. Air feeds fire and fire warms air. In fact, fire requires air. However, not all air and fire combinations work. I have included information about the different birth periods within each star sign and this will throw even more light on your prospects for a fulfilling love life with any star sign you choose.

Good luck in your search for love, and may the stars shine upon you in 2013!

STAR SIGN COMPATIBILITY FOR LOVE AND FRIENDSHIP (PERCENTAGES)

	Aries	Taurus	Gemini	Cancer	Leo	Virgo	Libra	Scorpio	Sagittarius	Capricorn	Aquarius	Pisces
Aries	60	65	65	65	90	45	70	80	90	50	55	65
Taurus	60	70	70	80	70	90	75	85	50	95	80	85
Gemini	70	70	75	60	80	75	90	60	75	50	90	50
Cancer	65	80	60	75	70	75	60	95	55	45	70	90
Leo	90	70	80	70	85	75	65	75	95	45	70	75
Virgo	45	90	75	75	75	70	80	85	70	95	50	70
Libra	70	75	90	60	65	80	80	85	80	85	95	50
Scorpio	80	85	60	95	75	85	85	90	80	65	60	95
Sagittarius	90	50	75	55	95	70	80	85	85	55	60	75
Capricorn	50	95	50	45	45	95	85	65	55	85	70	85
Aquarius	55	80	90	70	70	50	95	60	60	70	80	55
Pisces	65	85	50	90	75	70	50	95	75	85	55	80

In the compatibility table above please note that some compatibilities have seemingly contradictory ratings. Why, you ask? Well, remember that no two people experience the relationship in exactly the same way. For one person a relationship may be more advantageous, more supportive than for the other. Sometimes one gains more than the other partner and therefore the compatibility rating will be higher for them.

HOROSCOPE COMPATIBILITY
◎ FOR PISCES ◎

Pisces with		Romance/Sexual
Aries		There is powerful sexual chemistry at work here; fire and water create steam
Taurus		There will be a sizzling sexual relationship between the two of you
Gemini		You don't understand each other very well and it would be hard to get this relationship off the ground
Cancer		You are emotionally compatible, caring and supportive; a great match

Friendship	Professional
✔ You have different approaches to social activities, but you can have a wonderful friendship	✘ Your laid-back attitude may annoy Aries; this will spill over into the finances and they won't be impressed
✔ Astrologically compatible; a great friendship	✔ A successful business partnership can be formed
✘ Gemini doesn't understand your sensitivity or style of communication	✘ Not enough substance for a successful business partnership
✔ You can be friends as well as lovers, which is quite unique	✔ You are a mutual support system and could build a wonderful business career together

Pisces with		Romance/Sexual
Leo		The emotional and sexual energies between you are unusual, but it could work
Virgo		Opposites do attract, but the relationship doesn't always go the distance; Virgo can be too critical for you
Libra		You will either love each other or be totally confused by your different communication styles
Scorpio		Scorpio can offer you undying love; a special and magical match that others will envy

Friendship	Professional
✗ Leo will bolster your self-esteem and you, in turn, will give loving support	✔ With focus and hard work, you can achieve great things together
✗ Not a great basis for friendship as Pisces will tire of Virgo's search for perfection	✗ If you leave the money issues in Virgo's hands and take care of the creativity, this could work
✔ Librans are party people, but they also need their space, just as you do, Pisces	✗ Your combined personalities could forge a successful business partnership
✔ You understand each other on so many levels	✔ Keep your emotions in check if you intend to go into business with Scorpio

Pisces with		Romance/Sexual
Sagittarius		Intimate relationships are well favoured in this match; there are a lot of sexual and emotional aspirations in common
Capricorn		Capricorn will appreciate your patience and the security you bring to the relationship
Aquarius		A powerful blend of the emotional and the intellectual; good sexual chemistry
Pisces		Who better than your own star sign to have a relationship with? Instant understanding is the prize

Friendship	Professional
✔ The stars favour a friendship between these two signs; you really understand each other	✘ You have a different approach to money issues; this will need to be sorted out before you sign on the dotted line
✔ You are opposites, but you could still forge a wonderful friendship	✔ Capricorns can work hard and are good at taking care of the finances; you would benefit from their knowledge
✘ Aquarius needs to put all their cards on the table so you know exactly what their game is	✔ If you want a professional life spent living on the edge, team up with an Aquarian
✔ It's fine to make sacrifices, but just ensure you don't become the unwilling victim of a scam	✘ The boundaries need to be clear and well defined before you go into a business relationship with another Piscean

◎ PISCES PARTNERSHIPS ◎

 Pisces + Aries

You both create a strong impression and have reasonably good sexual attraction, but there are some essential differences that need to be addressed. Pisces, you are sensitive and may find it hard to handle the abrupt and independent attitude of Aries. You are more considerate of people's feelings and Aries may find this hard to understand.

 Pisces + Taurus

Pisces is a little more ethereal than the practical Taurus. You'll have to prove to Taurus that a balance is possible. Taureans are skeptical, but you can teach them a lot about trust and opening up their hearts to a deeper and more emotional relationship and love.

 Pisces + Gemini

Gemini relates to the mind, whereas Pisces relates to emotions. If you want to bond deeply with each other,

Gemini has to show that they are sensitive to your non-verbal ways of communicating. A look or gesture can be as meaningful as words—once Gemini breaks the code.

Pisces + Cancer

Feeling is the operative word in a relationship between Pisces and Cancer. There is a strong bond between you as Pisces stimulates the emotionally intuitive side of Cancer. Feeling, touching and being demonstrative is something you have in common. You are also both considerate of the other and your sexual and intimate needs will be wonderfully satisfied.

Pisces + Leo

Leo is a warm and grounded sign that can either bring you gently down to earth or force you to crash land. Leo will offer you a greater level of self-esteem, especially if you happen to be a shy and retiring Piscean. Your gentle and loving support will be an asset to Leo in their search for success.

Pisces + Virgo

Opposites often attract, but you are both changeable and moody in your own way. Virgo is meticulous and wants to understand and categorise everything in detail. You, on the other hand, are happy to let nature take its course. Virgo may interpret this as a form of mental laziness.

Pisces + Libra

Pisceans, like the fish that represents them, swim in schools, and they enjoy social interaction. However, there are times when they prefer their own company. Libra may find this hard to understand and you will both need to make adjustments if this relationship is going to get to the next level.

Pisces + Scorpio

This match is one of those special and magical unions that most of us only dream about. It is a combination of powerful and emotional energies. Scorpio's practical approach is perfect for Pisces, particularly when they are off with the pixies. Being with a Scorpio will remind you of exactly why you were born.

Pisces + Sagittarius

This combination will be anything but ordinary. You are happy with a settled home life, whereas Sagittarius always seems to be going somewhere or has just arrived back. It will take them a long time, if ever, to be content with what you have to offer, Pisces.

Pisces + Capricorn

Capricorn finds you quite unusual, Pisces. You tend to live life with your heart rather than your mind, and you are constantly daydreaming. This can frustrate Capricorn as they feel you are not doing anything practical to firm up your relationship as a couple. You are not entirely compatible, but you could still build a lasting relationship.

Pisces + Aquarius

Aquarius is somewhat offbeat for you, Pisces, and they think things through in a bold and progressive way. You could feel undermined if you're not prepared to change and adapt to their unique and idealistic personality. This is an unusual combination, but a little give and take on both sides could make it work.

Pisces + Pisces

Who better to understand you, Pisces, than another Piscean? The emotional and sensitive energies that you combine in this relationship can result in a downpour of loving rapture and ecstasy if you're developed and grounded enough to organise yourselves as a couple. This relationship could be a great and undying love.

PLATONIC RELATIONSHIPS: BEST AND WORST

BEST PAIRING:
PISCES AND TAURUS

Pisces and Taurus can become excellent friends, and this will be evident at their first meeting. Pisces, being the eleventh sign of the zodiac to Taurus, is an area of fulfilment for Taurus. This promises great friendship and an ability to fulfil them in what they aspire to do.

Pisces is a little less grounded than Taurus; some might even say they have their head in the clouds. Taurus, who is the practical one in the relationship, will want proof of whatever you say. There is a balance possible, Pisces —if you can keep your feet on the ground.

Taurus can teach you the value of balancing your idealistic and practical duties on a day-to-day basis. This may be tough for you at first, but if you persist, the two of you can learn a lot from each other, and together you can accomplish something of value in this world.

Taurus is very different to you, Pisces, because they are straightforward in many respects. They are complex individuals and like to look at life and its meaning from many different angles. Your main aim is to understand life and find out what makes the world go around. Their spiritual perspective is very practical, while yours doesn't have to be so functional or tangible.

Taureans are not known for their speed in making up their mind, and you may run out of patience with them at times. You like to look at life through a kaleidoscope and see many differing colours and shades. You want to comprehend the issues of life and even get to the heart of the mystery of life and nature itself.

You certainly have a lot in common, even though you are a water sign and Taurus is an earth sign, and you will feel comfortable in each other's company. Taurus is often content with more routine aspects of existence, whereas you tend to be a daydreamer. Security is very important to them, and they like to know from one day to another where everything is and what's to be expected. They don't especially like surprises, either.

However, Taurus will open up a whole new world for you with new experiences, entertainment and cultural activities. You will really enjoy this part of your friendship with them.

WORST PAIRING:
PISCES AND LEO

In a friendship with Leo, there will be very wide gaps in your lifestyles and personality traits. With the combined influence of water and fire, the elements that rule you respectively, this is not an easy relationship to deal with.

You are the last sign in the zodiac, Pisces, and you are a selfless and compassionate human being. Leo, on the other hand, put themselves first, and there will be times when you will be doing all the giving and Leo all the taking. They are strongly preoccupied with the idea of showing off their personality and developing their ego, both for social and material benefits. For a time you will go along with this because you are a very generous human being, but it will reach a point when you will get fed up with them.

Leo is a fixed sign and their opinions can be inflexible. You will find it difficult to express yourself freely with someone who nit-picks everything that you say. Even though your planets are astrologically friendly, there will be an underlying tension, and you may feel that Leo bullies you and doesn't allow you to have your say.

You tend to live in a fantasy world, Pisces, exploring the unknown in a tender and touching way. It is unlikely that Leo will allow you the space to keep your head in the clouds, and they will make you feel that you haven't really got it together. You may find it hard to reconcile your differences with the showy, 'look at me' Leo.

SEXUAL RELATIONSHIPS: BEST AND WORST

BEST PAIRING:
PISCES AND SCORPIO

The matching of Pisces and Scorpio is one of those special, almost magical, unions that most of us can only dream about. It is one of the most extraordinary love matches of the zodiac. Emotion, communication and unbridled passion are all special keywords that apply to your relationship.

There is a combination of powerful emotional energies in this relationship, and the key factor that makes it work is that you both want to show your feelings for each other. You understand each other so well that there is no difficulty in serving each other and meeting those needs that lead to a fulfilling and loving relationship.

You intuitively understand the complex Scorpio personality and know just how to touch them in body, mind and spirit. When Pisces works its way into the

Scorpio psyche, there's very little they can do except fall head-over-heels in love with you.

Two sensitive water signs can produce an overwhelming amount of uninhibited passion and love. Scorpio will ground you and tune into those intuitive powers so that a special attachment between you can be thoroughly developed. You have the uncanny knack of being on your Scorpio partner's wavelength. You can become attached to each other very quickly and your passion and emotions will head for the heavens.

To a Piscean-born individual, Scorpio possesses the wizard's touch in being able to draw them back from a seemingly disconnected world in which they forget the practical aspects of day-to-day life. Once they commit to you, there will be no turning back.

AN INTUITIVE BOND

Your Scorpio partner will be amazed at your uncanny knack for knowing what they are feeling. As one of the most brooding signs of the zodiac, they will be astounded at your continuing ability to sense their pain and soothe it as well.

You both have strong intuitive powers and instinctively understand what the other is thinking without a word having to be spoken. You have the mutual ability to understand the deeper emotional lives that you want, and are able to open your hearts and minds to each other and share your deepest feelings. This goes a long way towards creating a mutually satisfying sexual relationship.

You can have a wonderfully fulfilling relationship because you are so tuned in to each other. Even if your Scorpio partner carries some emotional baggage from their past, you will be able to provide them with the love and understanding that they need to release these turbulent feelings. Once this special attachment has been created, you will find it almost impossible to be apart.

WORST PAIRING:
PISCES AND LIBRA

Your relationship with Libra will be difficult, to say the least. On the one hand, you'll be totally in love with them, but on the other hand, you'll feel confused and even resentful.

You're both very sociable, and you are comfortable with each other's company and the company of friends and family. But you, Pisces, need moments of solitude for your spiritual and emotional regeneration. It is unlikely that Libra will be sensitive to this, and they may see it as retreating from them emotionally. They won't understand that you are just recharging your batteries.

You both love to flirt, and this is okay, provided that you, Pisces, do not get too possessive. Your sexual appetites are quite different and you may end up irritating each other, which will affect your romantic life. If you put your foot down and disapprove of your Libran partner's romantic escapades, this is where your problems will begin.

Pisces, you run the risk of retreating back into your fantasy world when the real world gets too difficult. You can, of course, continue with this relationship, even though you are not happy, but you will be forever compromising, and the chances of you achieving a 50-50 balance are remote.

Librans are indecisive and you can become quite exasperated at their lack of leadership. If you are a Pisces woman, you need someone who can take responsibility in the family. Librans, especially in their younger years, avoid this path as they don't want to be tied down.

Librans talk a lot, usually about themselves, whereas you might not be so vocal, and their endless chit chat will drive you crazy. You will probably want them to be quiet at times, but they are better at talking than listening. You, on the other hand, communicate with your mind and heart, but your Libran lover will not get where you're coming from. They will feel that you are talking in riddles and won't bother trying to work out what you actually mean.

If you harbour dreams of perfection, unconditional love, selflessness and spiritual idealism, then you need to look somewhere else for a lifelong partner. Once your idealistic view of love is shattered, it will make it hard for you to look for romance again. So, if the going gets tough with Libra, then you might as well get going.

QUIZ: HAVE YOU FOUND YOUR PERFECT MATCH?

Are you game enough to take the following quick quiz to see how good a lover you are? The truth sometimes hurts, but it is the only way to develop your relationship skills.

It is no surprise to anyone that we are all searching for our soul mate, the modern version of the knight on a white horse or maiden in distress. In the hurly burly of life, we might bypass that special one all because we are not looking hard enough.

You may be in a relationship that started off with fireworks but that is now burnt out. When will you know if that happens and what will you do about it?

If you are in currently in a relationship, are you truly happy or just marking time until someone else comes along who suits you better? Are you content with just one partner, or would you rather play the field?

When you are without a partner, are you happy on your own or do you feel as though half of you is missing and just waiting to be joined up with someone new?

Are you in a situation where you just don't seem able to find anyone, let alone the perfect partner? Are you looking in the right places?

Pisces, you are the ideal lover who often makes the mistake of falling in love with the wrong partner. Your idealism sometimes blinds you to the reality of the person before you. If you're already in a relationship, it's important to analyse how well suited you are to each other.

So here's a checklist for you, Pisces, to see if he or she is the right one for you.

Scoring System:

Yes = 1 point

No = 0 points

❷ Does your partner value your dreams?

❷ Does your partner care for you romantically?

❷ Are they sensitive to your feelings?

❷ Does your partner share your vision of having a child someday?

❷ Does your partner always reassure you that you are the only one?

❷ Does your partner always tell you that they love you?

❷ Does your partner remember important and sentimental dates, like the day you met?

❷ Do they value your opinion?

❷ Does your partner value your traditions?

❷ Does your partner give you some time alone when you need it?

❷ Are you proud of your partner when you are introducing them to others?

❓ Do you visualise being with your partner in the future?

❓ Does your partner respect your sensitivity?

❓ When you are with your partner, do they make you laugh and engage you in deep conversation?

Have you been honest with your answers? Really? There is absolutely nothing to be gained here by tweaking the answers to suit the outcome. If you are aware that you are turning a blind eye to some things that are irritating or fall short of your expectations, then you will not get a real representation of your relationship.

Here are the possible points that you can score:

8 to 16 points

A good match. This shows you have obviously done something right. You have a partner who understands you, your life and your needs. But this doesn't mean you can just sit back and relax. There is always room to improve and make this excellent relationship even better.

5 to 7 points

Half-hearted prospect. You are going to need to work hard at this relationship. It may require some good honest dialogue between the two of you, and honesty is the keyword here. Go through the questions with each other and see what it is that's not allowing a better relationship to shine through. Is one of you too lazy or too domineering? After some time, do the quiz again and see if you rate your romance better. If not, it might be time to call it quits.

0 to 4 points

Washed up. There is insufficient mutual respect and understanding on this score. It's likely that neither of you is happy and that you have become too comfortable, like a worn-out pair of slippers. Is that what you want to be?

2013
YEARLY OVERVIEW

CHEERS TO A NEW YEAR AND
ANOTHER CHANCE FOR US TO
GET IT RIGHT.

Oprah Winfrey

◎ KEY EXPERIENCES ◎

Your home life is particularly important to you throughout 2013, and as Jupiter blesses you with increased satisfaction with your family and relatives, you will realise that being undistracted by problems on the home front will give you more energy to do the things you want to do personally and professionally.

This year, with Saturn passing through your zone of spirituality and ethics, you will be focused on reviewing your belief system, especially if it hasn't served you well on a practical level. This may not be easy, but if you get this issues clarified, the following 12 months will be extremely satisfying.

ROMANCE AND
◎ FRIENDSHIP ◎

This year will find you relying on friends and the opportunities they present to you to find meaning in your life. Understanding how others manage their relationships will also be of keen interest to you as Mercury and Pluto focus your attention on these important matters.

....

IMPROVE YOUR LOVE LIFE

In the first couple of months of 2013, you will be particularly interested in trying to understand relationships: what motivates you, what causes problems, and, of course, what you can do on a subtle level to improve your love life.

....

Because Jupiter will bring with it an expansive and happy phase for you, you will be able to give your best to the one you love. If you have not been fortunate enough to find your soul mate, I can say emphatically that the planetary positions indicate that you will be a little less awed by new situations, and that you will take every precaution to make sure that those you get involved with are worthy of your love.

Important developments for romance occur at the very end of June when Jupiter, along with the Sun and Mercury, trigger a whole new range of feelings and experiences for you. This is a lucky phase, and for the first time in 12 years, you will feel your confidence growing. At this time, the opportunity of meeting a high calibre soul mate is high.

As the year progresses, there will be further developments in your love life, and in July and August, when Venus transits your romance sector, you must be careful not to overinflate your estimation of someone you meet. Keeping your feelings real and, of course, not getting carried away by the superficialities of friendship and love, you will be on target to make this a year of learning, experience and emotional satisfaction.

 Relationships on the Rise

It is vitally important for you to make yourself available when invitations come rolling in after the 9th of January. Put yourself in the way of Cupid's arrow because this is a period when you will be meeting many new people. Between the 13th and the 20th, however, be on guard as your impulses are strong and the choices you make may not be based on sound assessments of human character.

After the 26th of February, when Venus transits your Sun sign, you will make further positive inroads in your love life. Up until the 12th of March, you will feel great and look good, too. It may also be time for a new makeover, or at least a period when you will pamper yourself and send out a clear message that you are worthy of love.

Sizzling hot romantic escapades occur when Venus traverses your zone of love after the 3rd of June. Although plenty of opportunities will present themselves, you must be careful as there are counteractive influences, such as that of Mars and Neptune on the 8th, Venus and Uranus on the 13th, and also Venus' movement to the sixth house of problems on the 28th. These dates require you to keep your wits about you and not be drawn into doing things you might otherwise regret.

Your thinking and expectations are big after the 22nd of July. You are not prepared to put up with anything less than what you consider to be the best, and with Mars and Jupiter being supported by Venus' transit in your marriage sector, the period between July and August should be memorable for you. You may even find yourself attracted to more than one member of the opposite sex.

Problems can arise when Mars enters your marital zone after the 15th of October. Try to maintain a cool head and keep the lines of communication open. These issues may continue up until the 15th of November. After this, the door of friendship can open again, but please don't be too impulsive or dominant in your relationships as this could create the opposite effect of what you are after.

WORK AND MONEY

Harness Your Moneymaking Powers

Making money can be summed up in an equation:

$$m \text{ (\$ money)} = e \text{ (energy)} \times t \text{ (time)} \times l \text{ (love)}$$

If one of the elements above is not functioning properly in your life, making money may become all the more difficult. With the way the world economy is going, you need to do everything you can to improve your chances of being financially independent and secure.

It's always necessary to gain an understanding of all the universal laws of abundance and success when dealing with money. When fully present and creative, you inject the spirit of enthusiasm and love in what you do, be it work or play, and your aura or electromagnetic appeal becomes so much stronger. It is a force that attracts people, opportunities and, of course, more money. Your destiny and karma can be significantly influenced by the way you think and the attitude you foster. This will in turn impact upon your moneymaking powers.

Pisces, with Uranus destabilising your financial zone, you must tread warily throughout the coming 12 months when it comes to finances, spending and earnings. Mars, your lucky planet, transits your expense zone as the year commences, and you are likely to overspend without even knowing it. Pace yourself at this early stage of the year, otherwise you will find yourself short on cash further down the line.

Investments in real estate seem to be favoured up until early July as Jupiter creates an expansive element to your personality. You may think of purchasing property, land or housing as a means of gaining a return on your money. On one level, this may work for you, but you certainly need to get appropriate advice and balance all factors before throwing big money in this direction.

You continue to be speculative, and with Jupiter, Mars and Mercury goading you on, you may feel that nothing you do can go wrong. But this could simply be a reflection of over-confidence and a lack of real knowledge about the things you wish to throw your money at. If you must have your head in the clouds, try to keep you feet on the ground.

September is a month when debts could be the cause of disputes and irritability for you. Try not to react to those who are simply advising you on how to better your finances. You can balance your impulses and financial drives with a constructive frame of mind after the 15th of September, when your innovation and hard work will yield good dividends.

On the 13th of October, and again on the 15th of November, you may be curious about how you can better your income or at least reduce your overheads to increase your savings. Talk to your bank manager or financial advisor about ways in which you can reduce the interest on your home payments or find a better deal on a credit card interest rate.

After the 22nd of November, and again on the 22nd of December, the Sun punctuates your yearly cycle with some great opportunities for bettering your professional status, which will in turn increase your financial prospects.

 Tips for Financial Success

It's possible to be thoroughly progressive and yet thrifty when it comes to money in the coming 12 months. A key tip to earning well and enjoying the benefits of an affluent lifestyle is coming up with new ideas and thinking outside the square. With Uranus spending several years in your finance sector, the keyword will be unexpectedness.

Throughout January, and again in April and May, you will be clever in coming up with new angles on producing work quickly and efficiently. You may not expect financial improvement, but you will be pleasantly surprised when Uranus brings you these unforeseen benefits.

On the 29th of March, the Sun and Venus, along with Mars and Uranus, occupy your finance sector, indicating a busy time and the opportunity for extra gains, but also the danger of excessive spending. An important tip for you at this time, and for the rest of the year, is to balance your impulses with good judgment.

When it comes to cutting a deal, you mustn't let the combined influence of Mars and the Sun create dissention and strife in your business relationships. It's best to delay any communication or negotiation until tempers subside.

When Venus comes to your eleventh zone of profits and fulfilment in November, there is the possibility of excellent profits for those of you who run a business. You should use the last months of the year to re-inject some of those profits into your business to grow it further.

 Career Moves and Promotions

Venus in the career zone is always a welcome astrological feature, and this is the case with you throughout 2013. The planet transits your zone of professional activities in January, but also throughout February, and offers you an additional dose of charm and personal magnetism that makes it easy for you to ask your boss or a third party for favours.

I would recommend that you put your best foot forward in the first two months of the year as it will be easy for you to acquire a new position, if that is what you desire. You will be intensely engaged up until the 17th of January, but after the 2nd of February, you may find yourself a little weary with work matters, so take a rest.

Contractual obligations between the 25th of April and the 6th of May herald a new period in your life, which means that it is a good time to seek professional improvement. On the 22nd of July, the 30th of July, the 1st of September and the 15th of September, you can aggressively seek a coveted position, either within your current employment or elsewhere. Don't waste time and don't be afraid to speak your mind as this will further your cause. You have a final opportunity to request a better position after the 22nd of November when the powerful solar energy dominates your horoscope, bringing with it good luck and enhanced reputation.

SPOTLIGHT ON VENUS

When Venus shines its beneficent rays on your career zone after the 2nd of July, you will start to feel more supported in your work and could even be nominated for a special role or position during this time.

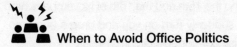

When to Avoid Office Politics

There may be an air of suspicion as the year starts due to the placement of the Moon in the sixth zone of work affairs and Mars in the secretive twelfth house. Although you feel reasonably comfortable in your workplace, there may be some underlying tension that you can't quite put your finger on. Trust your intuition, especially throughout the end of January and early February, when several planets indicate ominous or covert activities within your peer group of associates.

There can be open combat when Mars, in its hard aspect, challenges your workplace after the 8th of February. It may be easier to lash out, but bite your tongue as you may have a better opportunity to crush your enemies later in the year. Work quietly and hold any trade secrets or gossip close to your chest at this time. You will also have to deal with an adversary after the 28th of June. This person may appear to be rather sweet-tongued, but make no mistake about it: this person may have ulterior motives. Keep them at arm's length.

Around the 28th of July, the 28th of August and the 9th of September, you may find yourself distracted by adversaries and will need a stroke of genius to get them on-side. Around the 15th of September, however, Mars and Uranus may assist you in striking up a truce. Be careful around the 15th and the 16th of November when friends may suddenly turn on you and drop a bomb on your otherwise comfortable circumstances.

HEALTH, BEAUTY AND
⊚ LIFESTYLE ⊚

 Venus Calendar for Beauty

Venus sets the trend for an excellent year, especially in showing others what you are capable of in the first quarter of 2013. It is the most elevated planet at the start of the year, and as it transits the apex of your horoscope, you can rely on it to help you get through any difficult times this year.

GOOD VIBRATIONS

An excellent trend is forecast for you from the 26th of February. These excellent vibrations assist you not only in your social affairs, but also in more serious matters at home where you may need an extra shot of diplomacy to solve some long-standing problems.

There is a strong creative impulse that is very marked from the 3rd of June. If possible, you should set aside time, even pulling away from work, to showcase your creative and expressive abilities. This is not so much to win the attention or affection of anyone, but to give you a sense of deep inner spiritual satisfaction. Beauty, of course, starts on the inside.

Watch your health after the 2nd of July as work could be placing a strain on you. This will show in your physical features, including your complexion and the elasticity of your skin. Listen to your body's signals as this is a barometer of your health. Increase your vitamin intake and naturally observe the reaction of your body to different types of food, alcohol and environments.

When Venus enters your zone of marriage after the 22nd of July, it's all systems go, and your confidence will reach another mini peak. You will be brimming with happiness, and this will spill over into your relationships.

What was commenced at the beginning of the year can come to fruition after the 8th of October when Venus once again traverses your zone of career. This same zone is considered the pinnacle of one's ego development. You are only as beautiful as you feel, and from now until December, it's likely you will feel great about yourself.

 Showing off Your Pisces Traits

Each Zodiac sign has its own unique power based upon the elements and planets that rule it. Unfortunately, most people don't know how to tap into this power and bring out their greatest potential to achieve success in life.

The greatest attribute of Pisces is the ability to show compassion to all equally. Venus, the planet of love,

Learn to Discriminate

Discrimination is an important keyword for you throughout 2013. Shower your blessings on those who will appreciate what you have to give them.

shows that this characteristic is fully expressed through your work and public affairs in 2013. As I've said to many Pisces clients over the years, it's fine to exhibit compassion and generosity, but be careful not to waste this valuable resource on people who are undeserving.

Your other wonderful star sign trait relates to spiritual insights and intuitive responses to life and the people around you. Between the 7th of February and the 15th of April, you will feel a quickening of your spirit, and these impulses will allow you to bypass the processes of the brain to gain a direct understanding of people's intentions and what will happen in the future.

It's one thing to have these spiritual and intuitive impulses, but quite another to know how to act upon them. This involves a process of trust. In other words, trust yourself and the promptings that arise within your heart. This will require practice over the coming year.

In the later part of the year, especially from the 17th of October and the 22nd of December, your affectionate nature will win you a few extra brownie points as well. You can share this aspect of your star sign with friends and strangers alike.

 Best Ways to Celebrate

This is a rather unusual year for you, Pisces, because there are some indications that you will take pleasure in earning money, and that you will celebrate life by measuring your joy and happiness by how much you earn. Because Mercury, the Sun and Pluto are positioned in your eleventh zone of Capricorn, which relates to your life's ambitions and friendships, this can be done with the help of friends.

One of the most satisfying arenas in which you can party, entertain and generally share your joy is in the immediate confines of your own home. This is because of the placement of Jupiter in the intellectual and entertaining sign of Gemini. There will be a great deal of activity in this area of your life, and it will continue unabated until Jupiter exits your zone of home affairs in the middle of the year.

Some sort of important celebrations may take place after the 27th of June. This could have to do with children or youngsters, either the birth of your own children or those of relatives. In any case, it will be a time for you to share in the pleasure of youth, innocence and the expansion of the family.

KARMA, SPIRITUALITY AND EMOTIONAL ◉ BALANCE ◉

You may need to deal with some past karmic issues this year as the planet Saturn and the north node transit your ninth house of past actions. For many Pisceans, going back in time and analysing their actions and the consequences of those actions will be of primary importance.

Mars is a key planet transiting the zone of hidden secrets. Releasing yourself from guilt or shame is critical to relieving you of the burdens that can inhibit your happiness this year. After the 2nd of February, you may find that a lot of the work that I am referring to is pretty much done, but then comes the hard work of applying your wisdom to the day-to-day affairs of your life.

The Moon rules your future karma and finds itself in your zone of health, deaths and enemies. You may have several sudden or unexpected turning points in your approach to health and work, and these two areas of your life are likely to be connected. Look at how these areas are hindering or helping you. It may also say something about your attitude towards your life—what you have, what you don't have and what you fear you might lose. Remove all of these thoughts from your mind and rest assured that a feeling of gratitude is the key to attracting wealth, happiness and good karma in your future.

SPIRITUAL EVOLUTION

A karmic turning point for you is the transit of Jupiter in the fifth zone or future karma segment of your horoscope in June, which will have a marked and positive influence on your spiritual evolution.

After the 26th of June, you will feel a distinct shift in energy, particularly if, leading up to this date, you felt frustrated by things moving slowly or not getting what you want or deserve in life. Hang on to your seat because things will change and you should prepare yourself for an exhilarating rollercoaster ride of ups and downs, but mainly ups after this date.

2013

MONTHLY & DAILY PREDICTIONS

IF YOU DON'T LIKE SOMETHING,
CHANGE IT; IF YOU CAN'T CHANGE
IT, CHANGE THE WAY YOU THINK
ABOUT IT.

Mary Engelbreit

❂ JANUARY ❂

 Monthly Highlights

You can expect some intense activities within your circle of friends this month. Between the 10th and the 12th, during the phase of the New Moon, a new friendship may be formed that could cause a change in your attitude to others. By the 26th you may need some quiet time, but you will find that some long-forgotten projects still need to be completed.

---

1 There are wonderful opportunities to earn cash right now. Friends and money go hand in hand. A project of a social nature can be profitable.

---

2 There is no need to live in the shadow of your partner. You should assert yourself and make sure that the relationship is one of equality.

---

3   You could feel frustrated by bureaucrats and pen-pushers today. You want action, but you may be hindered. Patience is your keyword today.

4   You may be offended by someone's remarks, but you could be overreacting. Read between the lines before accusing anyone.

5   You are relentless in your pursuit of an objective and have lots of physical drive to make your dreams a reality.

6   Balance the inner and the outer, but make sure that what you are aspiring to is practical. Don't go to extremes; follow the middle path.

7   Stand up for what you believe in today and don't be vague about your philosophical beliefs. You may be challenged.

8   The key people you work with may not be amenable to your ideas. You need solid factual support to get others on side today.

9   Freedom at any cost is the catch-cry at present. You don't want to be bound by anyone and need space to breathe.

10 You could be reactive today, so it is best to slow down, take a couple of breaths and maintain your equilibrium before going into battle.

11 If you've been obstructed recently, now is the time to move forward and be positive about achieving some desired objective. Extra money could come your way.

12 You are learning new things, but could have the occasional mental blank. Don't let this deter you from self-improvement.

13 You need to hold off from making any important decisions today. Being left alone is the best way for you to gain some clarity.

14 You feel more in tune with yourself, so you should express this in your relationships. People will be more likely to pay attention to what you have to say.

15 You could be wasteful today and spend money on something you don't really need. Check with your partner or run it by a friend before committing yourself to a purchase.

16 Your mind is on financial matters and you need to find a better way of earning more money. Perhaps you need to reduce your expenses.

17 You will feel frazzled today because you are doing too many things. Stop, re-evaluate and set a realistic schedule for yourself.

18 You could feel sentimental today, maybe even a little teary. Revisiting the past or rummaging through old photographs could be exactly what you need to do right now.

19 You are muddled in your thinking and the planets are not helping you gain any clarity. Misunderstandings are likely. Travel is on the agenda and you want to get out and about.

20 You may have nothing in particular to do, but simply moving around will make you feel better.

21 Today is a day of intensity, and you could have difficulty trying to elicit the right sort of response from friends.

22 Don't try too hard, and allow people their own pace. You want to do more but don't have the physical energy. Listen to the signals in your body and rest if you need to.

23 Domestic issues take precedence right now as a family member requires your assistance. Give them the time they need, otherwise the issue will play on your mind.

24 You have excellent communication skills today, and any form of lecturing, advertising, sales or marketing is right up your alley. Use this power to your advantage.

25 Romance is in the air once again, and the Moon causes you to reach out to someone who may understand your feelings. This could be the start of a new romance.

26 A gamble is fine as long as it is based on fact and not a fleeting impulse. If you don't listen to your head and act with your heart, you may be in for a loss.

27 Your emotions may be cool at the moment, so try to explain this to someone before they misinterpret your attitude. Distance may be a good thing today.

28 Health matters take precedence and you may not feel up to par. If that is the case, a check-up is nothing to be alarmed about, just a precautionary measure.

29 A journey you had planned may have to be postponed due to unforeseen circumstances. This can always be revived in the future, so don't be too downhearted about it.

30 You may need more input from your significant other. Perhaps it's time for a heart-to-heart discussion.

31 Your communication style is greatly appreciated by people, friends and strangers alike. You could strike up a new friendship under this transit.

◉ FEBRUARY ◉

Monthly Highlights

Some unexpected good fortune in your finances can trigger new business activities. With Jupiter transiting your zone of domestic activities, they may tie in with real estate or speculations of this nature. Be careful of your expenditure this month as the Sun and Mercury move through your zone of unbridled spending. Meditation and spiritual activities seem to be part of your growth process just now, and between the 8th and the 15th you may find yourself actively working on this inner part of yourself.

1　Even if you don't play by the rules today, no one is going to particularly care. Lucky you! Enjoy your new-found power and freedom.

2　Your imagination is soaring today, but it may also be connected to spiritual matters. This is an excellent time to meditate and delve into the mysteries of life.

3   You have some psychic abilities at the moment, and you should trust them where others are concerned. If you don't, you may kick yourself later.

4   You may feel out of sorts and can't quite figure out why. This is just one of those transits that you need to experience without too much judgment.

5   You are interested in achieving more in your work and could be somewhat emotional about professional matters. Try to be business-like in your dealings.

6   The pace speeds up when Mercury enters your Sun sign. You're also humorous and able to multitask. You'll be so busy that others may not be able to keep up.

7   You want to do something creative but may lack the requisite skills. The solution is to learn some art form that will enable you to express yourself.

8 You are challenged in your working life, either by the job itself or people around you. Communication may not flow freely, so you need to express your thoughts through emails or the written word.

9 Dealing with someone from your past—perhaps an old flame—may be nerve-racking, but it is still something you wish to do. Draw a line in the sand and venture forth.

10 A big plan needs careful preparation. Unfortunately, you may not have done enough groundwork and, as a result, things may not work out.

11 Females you deal with may not be compliant or conducive to your manner of doing things. You will need to compromise today.

12 Your thinking is slow today, and facts, figures and other important data may not flow easily. It's best to have notes handy.

13 You can be more industrious today, especially where finances are concerned, and this includes being a little more disciplined. Watch your pennies and your dollars will look after themselves.

14 You could be thinking about something over and over again, like a cracked record. You need to relax and take your mind off the problem.

15 Someone in your peer group is demanding, and this is pushing you further and further away. You are not being honest for fear of jeopardising your relationship. Speak your mind.

16 You can successfully resolve a long-standing problem with a parent, possibly your father or a male relative. Once you have this out of the way, a load will be off your shoulders.

17 You could be invited somewhere that you find very uncomfortable. You'll remain polite, but you will not enjoy the experience.

18 If you are dynamic right now, you will continue to be so for the next few weeks as the Sun returns to Pisces. Enjoy your energy while it lasts.

19 You feel peaceful right now and will share this with others to bring them joy and satisfaction. Others may be looking to you for solutions to their problems.

20 You may commence a new relationship or friendship under the New Moon. But don't be too rash as all that glitters is not gold.

21 You have a desire to develop your ethics and philosophical understanding. Attend lectures and meet with others who have a handle on this sort of thing.

22 Your debts could spiral out of control over the coming days. If you tighten your belt, your credit card bills will be much leaner.

23 The pace at which you are working today is not up to standard. You may have to take some work home.

24 Your mind is on matters of love. If you are married, this could be a time when you need to reaffirm your vows to each other. You may be feeling some sort of lack.

25 An issue can be resolved, but it may have an impact on loved ones. Look for ways to resolve these issues with minimal damage.

26 Don't be too angry with others. You need to be a little more thoughtful in your friendships. Try to compromise.

27 You'll probably jump to a conclusion that may be incorrect. Think carefully before offering your opinion today.

28 A spiritual approach may be the right solution today. Don't think with your head. Use your intuition.

⊚ MARCH ⊚

Monthly Highlights

This is an extraordinarily intense month as six planets are impacting on your personal life. What this means is that you will be so busy that you could run yourself ragged, and the intensity of this is shown by the placement of the Moon in your zone of private sufferings, difficult personal relationships, etc. You need to take control and prioritise your activities or you may find yourself chasing your tail.

There are some excellent career opportunities, especially if you are looking for work after the 18th. Put your best foot forward and don't be afraid to attend interviews, even if you don't feel experienced enough.

Try not to be too obsessive about your relationships on the 31st. You may be imagining things that are not there.

1   You are sending mixed signals to others. Although you are attractive right now, try to keep it real. You don't want others misinterpreting you.

2   You may have been unclear about making changes, but today you will come to the conclusion that it is necessary. Go full steam ahead!

3   It may be necessary to upgrade equipment like computers, mobile phones, etc. Here comes another bill!

4   You may find yourself in the company of those who are negative, even though you have a positive, can-do attitude yourself. Pay no attention to them.

5   You want to help everyone today, but you will find yourself spread very thinly indeed. Stick to your own tasks.

6   You do not trust yourself right now, and this means you are likely to falter in your decision-making process. Get back to an instinctive understanding of things.

7 You have a desire to improve your personal circumstances and living space. Get down, roll up your sleeves and clear out the clutter.

8 You have a lot of emotional energy today, but you don't know where to put it. Being creative is an excellent way to redirect this power into positive channels.

9 Don't project your ill feelings on others. It's always best to look at yourself and how your life is unfolding. Take responsibility.

10 You are financially aggressive at the moment, and this may result in disputes with the ones you love. A conciliatory attitude is necessary today.

11 Financial issues continue to bother you, and you're likely to jump the gun and do something against the will of your partner. Think again.

12 It's an excellent time for contracts and getting what you want in business. For those who run an independent commercial enterprise, you'll do well just now.

13 Don't be so insular in your relationships and friendships. Being inclusive of others helps relationships grow. Invite others into the inner sanctum.

14 Pay more attention to your health and rebuild your sense of wellbeing. This requires discipline. Get started today.

15 Someone who made a promise may go back on their word. You will feel let you down, but you must understand that it is human nature.

16 Be clear about your intentions or someone may misinterpret what you are doing. It's not a bad idea to put things in writing at this time.

17 Concentration may be difficult as you are distracted by other things. It is best to solve a problem quickly if you don't have the mental power to stay focused.

18 You have a keen eye for detail and will make excellent improvements and corrections to the projects you are working on.

19 An employer may offer you something, only to go back on their word. You may feel disappointed by this turn of events, but it is best to ignore it.

20 It's time to let the inner child shine out from within you, even if others think it's a little silly. Follow your own truth and don't be afraid to try something new.

21 Looking at the past is only useful if you learn from your mistakes. You mustn't allow self-pity to undermine you.

22 You'll enjoy doing a back flip, especially if it's in retaliation to someone who has let you down recently. Be careful, though, or it could turn into a vicious cycle.

23 You could find yourself with a feeling of independence, especially if you have distanced herself from a friend or peer group. You've outgrown someone.

24 If someone is offering you an incentive, you need to get them to commit, preferably in writing.

25 Observing the way things are done in the workplace is a good way of learning. Book knowledge may fail you just now.

26 Get confirmation before you leave for an engagement or outing today. There may be a last-minute change of plans.

27 Being apart is sometimes sweet, especially if a relationship is getting complicated. Having time to get your thoughts together is a good idea just now.

28 Someone may be leading you down the garden path. Don't feel intimidated by their sweet talk. Put them to the test and ask them to prove that their offer is real.

29 Dealing with incompetence will have you seeing red. You will resent having to train someone who is in a superior position.

30 Make sure any romantic encounter is a sober one as you may do something you'll regret, or, worse still, that you don't remember.

31 You need to deal with someone's immaturity today. Don't allow your mood to deteriorate and drop to their level.

❂ APRIL ❂

 Monthly Highlights

You are so passionate about living the high life that you may actually look at another line of income. Four planets are passing through your zone of income and money, and, more importantly, material values. Try not to be too impulsive as Mars and Venus may cause you to choose tasteless sexual partners that you may regret later. Wait until the 15th if you need to sign a contract as this will be favourable for you.

An eclipse occurs in your zone of long journeys, which may reveal something to you about someone from afar. Your relationship with your father may also need to be explored.

1 Rough justice is sometimes necessary to keep the peace and bring everyone back in line. Today you may try something different to keep the troops in order.

2   A mindless rival may be dishing out nonsense. It's a battle of wits to get your point across today.

3   Unfortunately, it's a commercial world and everything revolves around the almighty dollar. You need to get used to this and step in with these protocols today.

4   Using your charm will be a way of fascinating your audience, especially if you're in some sort of sales-orientated career. This will bring maximum benefits to you.

5   A subject is certainly worthy of enquiry, even if at present you don't think it has much utility. Remain open-minded to what is on offer today.

6   You could receive a negative reaction to a request you have made to a superior. Perhaps they are not clear on what you want. Spell it out.

7   If you go into a meeting armed with a different comparison, you will get your ideas across more efficiently. Step outside the square.

8 What you need to do today is use enlightened focus and reasoning. You will be dealing with people who do not understand your point of view and who lack intellectual insight. Your job is to show them how it's done.

9 You will feel vulnerable if you allow yourself to become too dependent on someone right now. It's better to develop your independence.

10 A great balancing act is necessary today as you may be feeling out of whack. Do what you can to channel your energies into harmonious activities.

11 You may need to go undercover today to get something sorted out, especially if it is in the best interests of the group.

12 You're feeling a little paranoid about some upcoming plans in your work or social arena. If you don't say something, nothing will change.

13 You're feeling torn between work and home life. Once again, this is a time for creating balance in all areas of your life.

14 You may be concerned that money is vanishing from your wallet. Your first reaction is to suspect that it has been stolen, but it's your spending habits that are to blame.

15 Forgiveness is a virtue, both in others and yourself. This is your keyword today.

16 You're tired of the old ways and want a fresh change. Your consciousness is growing and you are seeking unique avenues of expression.

17 You may have trouble with your skeletal area or joints. Consider alternative treatments, such as osteopathy or chiropractic.

18 A crude or shocking headline creates a desire in you to do something more for the community or the world at large. Your altruistic temperament is strong today.

19 You may realise that your grades or general education are restricting you. It's never too late to learn. Look afield.

20 Being allocated a new position may help you gather momentum. Implementing changes may be a challenge.

21 Fortitude is your keyword today. You will need to deal with many challenges and responsibilities. Strength of mind is necessary.

22 You can't just get to your destination overnight. Protracted work, sweat and, sometimes, tears are necessary. Remember that.

23 Looking too gorgeous can actually have the opposite effect. You may attract the wrong sort of attention, so be careful.

24 You could be touched by a note or gesture from a friend or stranger today. Karma arises when you least expect it.

25 Don't be afraid to express your skepticism if someone is not making sense. You will soon extract the truth out of them.

26 Your partner could become unfriendly if you decide not to accompany them somewhere today. The eclipse is clouding their mind.

27 Until you make it, fake it. This may be the case at work, especially if you skills are not up to scratch. This is not dishonesty, just creativity.

28 Retail therapy could reach high intensity now as you use it as a means of blowing off steam. Share your experience with a friend.

29 Fixing your car or performing other service-related chores may take more time than you expected. Factor this into your day.

30 An unsuspecting recipient of your courtesy may be mistrustful of your motives. Reassure them.

◎ MAY ◎

 Monthly Highlights

You will be at odds this month over what to do about your lifestyle or residence. Whatever you're planning, it may not come easily as Saturn opposes several planets this month. Patience is your greatest virtue, especially after the 14th, when confusion may reign.

Some clarity on home affairs is bound to emerge after the 21st when the Sun moves through your zone of family life. The conjunction of Venus and Jupiter is fortuitous on the 29th. You may receive a gift or give something of value to someone.

1 An anticipated event may turn out to be anticlimactic. You need to take more control of outings like this in the future.

2 The forbidden may seem attractive today. If you've missed out on experiences earlier in your life, this is to be expected.

3   Be careful of environmental hazards just now. If you are painting, redecorating or working with chemicals, take adequate precautions.

4   Working within a conventional organisation may be frustrating right now. You have to find ways to make the routine fun and interesting.

5   If you are a driver, be careful not to speed. You could get booked if you thoughtlessly speed without consideration for the legal consequences.

6   A hassle with someone will be worth the effort as you will come out on top.

7   It is not the title that matters but the money you make. Don't be afraid to take on an optional role if it could work to your advantage.

8   Your prerequisites for an agreement have not been met. Because of this, it is in your best interests to revoke the deal.

9   A speedy romance is suggested, but whirlwind love affairs have a low rate of success. Remember this.

10 You may not necessarily trust your boss, but you will have to make an exception. They may be cagey at the moment.

11 Trust your intuition if someone is offering you a speculative opportunity that seems suspicious. What seems too good to be true usually is.

12 If you are not feeling well today, it is best to postpone an outing, especially if you'll be in an unusual environment.

13 You can reclaim a sense of love and respect in your relationship only if the feeling is mutual. Avoid one-sided affairs.

14 You see pitfalls for your children or those less experienced, but remember that life experience is the best teacher.

15 You may hear of a birth and will be asked to join in the celebrations. Another cost? Gifts are inevitable.

16 You may be starved of mental activity and the onus is on you to stimulate this aspect of your being. Get to it!

17 Someone pulled a dishonest trick on you some time ago and now they've resurfaced. Once bitten, twice shy.

18 You are scattering your energies in many directions now. Redefine your path and objectives.

19 Don't take a position for granted. You will only be granted leeway by notifying the authorities of your intentions, especially if you intend to take time off.

20 To improve your relationships, you need to implement a revolution of sorts. If laziness or apathy has set in, today's the day to drop the bomb.

21 You may feel insecure and uncomfortable lending money to someone who is requesting it. Declining is the best way to keep a friendship intact.

22 You may need to go solo today, especially if you're tired of everyone pulling you this way and that. It's quite all right to have your own mind.

23 Someone's loyalty may seem repulsive today, especially if you realise that they are simply paying lip service. Play the game.

24 Regardless of the stress you are experiencing, keep your mind on the positive aspects of what you are doing. All is well.

25 To increase your wellbeing, you need to modify the atmosphere of your environment. Music can help.

26 You feel that a newcomer on the scene may be devious. Communicating with them may be difficult if trust is lacking.

27 Maintain a steady pace today and you will be surprised at the amount of work you get done. You'll enjoy a well-deserved rest on completion.

28 Although you'll enjoy someone's company, there is a subtle annoyance attached to the relationship. You'll need to grin and bear it.

29 Although you're worried about missing out on buying something scarce, don't worry; the object is not yet extinct. Look elsewhere.

30   Even popularity can place you under stress. Know when enough is enough. This is a case of ego versus wisdom.

31   Reviewing your friendships, and, more importantly, your love affairs, is essential. Be prepared for the unexpected.

☙ JUNE ❧

 Monthly Highlights

You are thinking about love this month, but divided loyalties could make it difficult for you to find the time. You will need to be shrewd to manage family affairs as well as a new love affair. Miraculously, things may move smoothly between the 7th and the 12th, but after the 13th your first impressions may take a sharp turn. Don't rush anything to do with love this month.

1 Even though you are not responsible for a problem today, you will become the fall guy. You need to cop it on the chin.

2 Your forecasts of what is coming may not be received well, but they will be correct. Stick to your guns today.

3 Love could be forcing you to expend a lot of emotional energy. Make sure you are getting as much affection as you are giving.

4   Any statements by friends or family should not be taken out of context as this could create misunderstanding and confusion.

5   Your current romantic scenario cuts both ways, so don't expect to have your cake and eat it too.

6   Holding on to your personal dogmas may be funny to others right now. Play along with the jokes, even if you think the joke is on you.

7   Don't become embroiled in other people's disputes, even if your intention is to help them. Collateral damage is likely, and you are the collateral.

8   If you are being governed by someone who is lazy, your discretion is necessary to point out the error of their ways.

9   There may not be any material benefit attached to a goodwill gesture on your part, but at least you'll feel good about yourself.

10 You may be accustomed to a certain genre of music, fashion or food, but a colleague will help you expand your circle of interests today.

11   If work is being conducted by someone who is incompetent, you may have a battle on your hands. You can avoid this by providing clear written directions at the outset.

12   If your duty has been executed superbly, you may receive an uncommon accolade or award. This should boost your self-confidence.

13   An obligation requires considerable discipline on your part. Seeking the advice of someone more experienced will help you get through it.

14   There is nothing more frustrating than an unattended office or a pre-recorded voice if you are calling to request some help. You may need to spend some time handling a problem like this today.

15   Take care of your head, and especially your eyes. Get an optical check-up, if necessary.

16   Just because you are authorised to access information, it doesn't mean that you can't get someone to do it for you.

17   Leading from behind is a subtle and clever way to win the hearts of others. Understate your power to win the approval of co-workers.

18 Wandering can be a splendid way to while away the time and reduce anger. Promise yourself that you will not do anything other than relax.

19 You may want to help the underdog today if you perceive any inequality around you. This is part of your Piscean personality.

20 It's time to start restricting your bouts of inebriation, especially if you have a taste for alcohol and other mind-altering substances. Get clean.

21 Karaoke is a great way to kick your heels up and enjoy a few hours with friends. This is a time of celebration and joy.

22 A bragger is usually the most insecure member of the group. Help them understand this insecurity and you'll become good friends.

23 Even if others are against you today, you will finish your work. Being drawn into idle chitchat is a danger just now. Keep your focus.

24 Unsuccessful attempts do not mean you are a failure. You must see these experiences as a means of strengthening your resolve.

25 You could feel uncomfortable with someone, especially if it is a romantic interlude. A one-night-stand may offer you seductive time-out.

26 Last minute changes could leave you and everyone around you frazzled. Allow yourself enough time to give equal attention to all your tasks.

27 The feminine side of your personality is likely to emerge just now. You'll be generous with others, but be careful of those who may take advantage of this.

28 Your idealism allows you to work your magic today. You can turn nothing into something and heal someone's broken heart.

29 There is a cloud over your finances at the moment. This is the result of allowing someone else to take charge. Regain control.

30 Get back to simple needs rather than complicating your desires. If you do this, being happy will be easier than you think.

⊚ JULY ⊚

 Monthly Highlights

You may decide that you want to start a whole new creative path for yourself, and with the excellent placement of Jupiter, the Sun and Mercury in your zone of self expression, this is quite likely. Young children may also feature strongly in the affairs of your life, as will new lovers or the resuscitation of a current relationship. This is more pronounced after the 22nd, when Mars and Jupiter move into close conjunction. Big plans can be expected at this time.

1   You may not express the right view today, and you could be tempted to change it for the sake of saving face. There's no need to adjust yourself simply to be accepted.

2   You need intense concentration to complete a report, but you will find very little pleasure in doing it today. You need to focus on the benefits of this task.

3   You'll feel considerable resistance if someone meddles with the work you've done in good faith. You may need to confront them to resolve this.

4   You should anticipate an enquiry from someone who is demanding more than you are prepared to give. You need to reflect the same measure of scrutiny back to them.

5   You need space to move and room to breathe just now, especially if you're feeling confined. Part of what you're doing seems impractical, but you're wrapped up in it.

6   There is a lot of noise around you just now, but what you really want is a little quiet time. You should make yourself conspicuously absent today.

7   Sometimes we are placed in a predicament where we have to accept the umpire's ruling. However, you may feel that the umpire is extremely unsuitable and inexperienced today.

8   The New Moon ensures a lift in your spirits and a more adventurous approach to relationships. Again, this is the start of new things for you.

9   You could be concerned about someone's capacity to act on your behalf in a business transaction. You need to learn the art of delegation.

10   You are not ready to make a commitment, either in a relationship or to some activity that requires more time and energy than you can give. Decline.

11   There are a mixture emotions welling up within you—excitement, worry and hope. You need answers from the one you love to settle your feelings today.

12   It is best not to give a professional problem any more thought. Put the issue aside for a day or two and it will sort itself out.

13   You're going to miss vital clues because of your impulsiveness today. Listen to what is being said before making any assumptions.

14   An unhappy individual may enter your life just now. Be careful not to become the victim of the person you are trying to help. Give advice, but watch your time.

15 You'll get frustrated trying to mediate a problem for others who are not able to unite. You are not God and cannot fix everything.

16 In matters of the heart, something will transpire that you did not think possible. This has everything to do with your positive attitude.

17 Anticipated conflicts will not arise and things will go better than you had expected. Your creative enterprise will impress someone right now.

18 You may think that a couple of bills have been paid, only to find that you actually overlooked them. If you've been managing your money well, you should have nothing to worry about.

19 You're feeling completely burned out during this cycle, and you may feel mentally and emotionally dejected. Step back from your work and be objective.

20 You have a sense that someone is deceiving you, but you will discover that these ill feelings are simply your imagination. Something you were waiting for will finally arrive.

21 You have the capacity to implement a new approach in your work, which could turn out to be very lucrative for you and your employer.

22 Nothing can stop you once you've made up your mind. The only issue is that your concept won't be completed as soon as you would like.

23 You are carrying a heavy load today and may be overworked and overtired. But much to your satisfaction, the project you are working on will be completed on time.

24 If you are single, you could be torn between two potential lovers. There's no rush. Take your time.

25 You may end up inheriting someone else's work. This could be good or bad, depending on the other person's level of professionalism. Let's hope they were responsible workers.

26 There could be an expression of interest in your work, or you may come up with a brilliant idea. This may bring financial benefits in the future.

27 Because things are moving so slowly, you may end up lazy and disinterested in the work you have to complete. It is best to take the day off.

28 Someone may throw a spanner in the works today, which could confuse issues surrounding money and your profession. Don't lose your balance in the process.

29 You must not discard any lead or introduction that comes your way today. It will be a quality opportunity that must be investigated more fully.

30 You feel flirtatious just now, probably because your partner is not giving you the attention you deserve. Try flirting with them!

31 Don't allow yourself to be swayed in a direction that is not going to work for you. Try to learn a different way of saying no.

☙ AUGUST ☙

Monthly Highlights

You have high expectations for your relationships in August, which is evidenced by Venus in your zone of marriage. However, be careful to avoid arguments as Mercury and Mars make you somewhat arrogant in conversation. Let the other person lead before offering your opinions. Take care not to speculate too heavily around the 21st as a gamble may turn into a debt.

1 Your focus should be on reaching your goals today, but you are more interested in what's happening on the home front. Divided loyalties may be an issue right now.

2 You need to straighten out some misunderstanding with someone, but they may not be available. Try again later in the day.

3   You are scared to reveal something of yourself to either a lover or a friend for fear that they may not accept you. Honesty is your keyword today.

4   Because you are unable to enlist the assistance of others, you may throw caution to the wind and simply have a fun day.

5   You may be reminiscing about some heartache or lost romantic opportunity. Because of this, you may be fearful of entering into a new relationship and opening your heart.

6   You might be upset by some business partner who raises inappropriate issues at the wrong time. You need to take control and postpone any discussions.

7   You may be thinking of taking out an additional loan to help you with some debts. The best approach is to trade your way out of this problem.

8   Although you want to sneak away, pressing work issues may keep pulling you back. Complete your tasks and then enjoy some relief.

9 You may be romantically approached by someone who is completely inappropriate, either in age or class. Nevertheless, you will still feel flattered.

10 Having fun will be uppermost in your mind, but you will not be able to fulfil this desire as other problems will impinge upon you. Better luck next time.

11 You are chained to a situation that you must get out of. But how? You need to give this question serious thought in the coming weeks.

12 Your wish to travel may be fulfilled just now. An offer to journey with a friend will bring you great joy, even if you can't do it immediately.

13 You need to contemplate your next move rather than being rash and taking action. Consider your alternatives carefully.

14 Luck is with you just now, and you are planning to trust the laws of abundance. By worrying about debts and a lack of money, you are shooting yourself in the foot.

15 You need to get in touch with your body to feel better and make a greater impact on those who can help you achieve your goals. Pay attention to nature's signals.

16 It's time to remove the elements in your life that are holding you back, and you will realise that some of your dreams are completely impractical. Ruthlessness is your mantra today.

17 Although there can be improvement in your financial circumstances, you are still concerned about many things. Focus on the positive and do what you can to remove the debt.

18 You will finally be paid what is owed to you, but it could still feel as if you have been short-changed in the process. Loans to friends? Never again!

19 You have so many options available to you right now that your head is spinning. The easiest way to deal with this is to eliminate what is unnecessary.

20 The success you expect may come in a completely different form, much to your surprise. In any case, you can still enjoy self-fulfilment today.

21 You can either go into battle or approach a situation with a cool and calm style of communication. The latter will work wonders.

22 If you are married but not yet a parent, the thought of having children may be uppermost in your mind during this astrological cycle.

23 You're being asked to take on responsibilities that you're not clear about. It is best to ask for clarification or you run the risk of making some serious errors.

24 You are clever in finding out the truth, and with this you are armed to move to the next level of your game plan. Don't stop until you succeed.

25 A powerful person may want to befriend you, but you will realise that there are strings attached to the arrangement, which will make you feel very uncomfortable.

26 You could be torn over making a decision and being asked to change it. The best course of action is to remain inflexible. Trust your intuition on this.

27 You may be nearing your goal, but something will cause you to vacillate and possibly change direction. Complete what you started before digressing.

28 Although you may win an argument today, you could be left with a bitter aftertaste and possibly some guilt. Reconciliation may be necessary.

29 When one door closes, another opens. Crying over spilt milk is not going to help you now. Move boldly forward with whatever decision you made.

30 You could be left in limbo by someone who is not offering you straight answers. You may need to proceed without them.

31 Legal matters may present some time-consuming problems. There's nothing that you can't work through systematically.

◎ SEPTEMBER ◎

Monthly Highlights

You could make a strong impression on the people you meet this month, particularly between the 4th and the 12th. Any business, sales or marketing activities you are planning will yield excellent results. If you are putting something up for sale, you will receive a good review and positive feedback from others. Good karma, luck and self-satisfaction will occur between the 22nd and the 30th.

1 You'll make an impact by stepping out from the crowd. By the same token, be patient and listen to what others have to say.

2 You may be thinking big today, but don't forget that you still need to attend to the details of what you are doing right now. Without this, success may not be yours.

3   You may be trying too hard to control relationships. Why not allow unions to grow organically and simply enjoy the process as it unfolds?

4   There may be difficulty communicating with someone who has shut down. Give them space before approaching them again.

5   Don't try too hard to impress your employer, especially if you're not clear on the subject matter. You must not let your ego dictate your actions today.

6   You mustn't allow fear to interfere with the opportunity to move forward in your life. Accept what is on offer, even if you don't feel up to the task.

7   This is a day of transformation, particularly in relation to your emotions and past experiences. Be honest enough to admit your own mistakes.

8   You will be uninterested in relationships today and more focused on money. Don't let materialism distract you from the true meaning of life.

9   You may spend money on something, only to realise later that it was not the right colour or size. You will need to spend time changing the item.

10   You may feel temporarily cut off from your peer group because you are not able to give them the attention that they demand just now. You'll need to explain your current responsibilities.

11   If you're confused by a situation that is impossible to resolve, let it go for now. Perhaps someone else can help you with it.

12   Your partner may not approve of the friends you are hanging out with, and this could cause friction. You need to bring the two parties face-to-face so that the issue can be put to bed.

13   Unfortunately, you can't be with the one you love just now, and this may cause you to feel dejected. Remember, however, that absence makes the heart grow fonder.

14   You are focusing too much on your own negative thoughts rather than being content with all that is good in your life. You can turn this around if you want to.

15 Someone may leave you hanging for a decision. For fear of irritating them, you are not pushing hard enough. Speak up or you will be victimised by this individual.

16 You are juggling too many balls in the air to satisfy everyone. It's time you did something for number one—and without any guilt attached to it.

17 You want to help a friend or relative in need, but your own circumstances may hinder you. There may be other ways you can help them. Be creative about this.

18 You may want more from your relationship and will feel bored with the same destinations and people. It's time for you to make some suggestions to change this.

19 Your emotions could go through a rollercoaster ride as you try to figure out the intentions of someone close to you. It appears that they are not respecting your feelings.

20 If you are still feeling emotional, this could interfere with your work and productivity. You need to be disciplined and put your emotions aside for the time being.

21 You may have grave doubts about a relationship today. You need to get confirmation from a third party to validate your concerns.

22 An outcome could be delayed, but this is no cause for depression. Quite the contrary. It will give you time for other projects.

23 There may be some invisible help, possibly some spiritual guidance, which will come to you in your time of need. By keeping the faith, you will get through this problem.

24 You will accept a request to help someone, but it will turn out to be more time-consuming than you had anticipated. There is a lesson in this for you.

25 You have some anxiety about your family budget and the way individual members are spending your hard-earned cash. This requires a family round-table discussion.

26 By fighting for what you believe in, even with clients, a dispute may turn out to be to your benefit. Your passion will count right now.

27 Sleepless nights will bother you, and you will wonder why things are the way they are. Worrying won't solve the problem. Work on a plan and stick to it.

28 You are concerned by someone's health, but you may not know what to do about it. You must understand that sickness is part of the karmic process.

29 If things have been slow, you may not be able to keep up with the pace of change that is happening right now. Remember, you must control the speed of things.

30 Someone may try to convince you to swerve from your path of righteousness—and you will refuse. This may fracture the relationship.

◎ OCTOBER ◎

 Monthly Highlights

Work colleagues could annoy you, so forbearance will be your keyword in the first few days of the month. Difficult aspects from the Sun and Venus also irritate you up until the 15th. A sudden meeting after the 17th could change your mood for the better—but don't be too quick to jump to conclusions. You may overlook a work commitment around the 24th, which could cause you to change plans abruptly.

1 Cash flow may be tight today, but overreacting to the situation is not going to give you a clear mind to find a solution. Don't get angry, just seek a logical answer.

2 Someone in your family may be an incredible burden right now. You have the opportunity to purify your spirit and do something that will elevate you to being a better human being.

3   If you keep compromising, you will never get what you want. You need to be somewhat ruthless in satisfying your needs and goals at this time.

4   You're only as good as your last hit, so people may be wondering whether or not you can prove yourself again. Now is the time to show them.

5   The laws of karma are operating in full force and you will start to see this in some of the results you are getting. After a period of giving yourself, you're now ready to receive in full measure.

6   You may find that you have a spiritual or social connection with someone you are conducting business with. Because of this, you will celebrate a new-found friend.

7   Someone younger and more enthusiastic than your usual group of friends will inspire you to step out of your usual circle. This will give you a new perspective on life.

8 Don't stay at home just because you feel obligated. If your desire is to spread your wings, you should do so and come back home refreshed.

9 If you have been trying to kick an old habit, your resolve will be much stronger now. Overcoming this problem will also put more cash in your pocket.

10 New changes in your work protocols promise exciting times ahead. However, you have to adjust to these new rules, which may not be easy.

11 A friend may move away or you may not have the same contact you used to. You will now appreciate them much more.

12 If something has to be postponed, don't worry. You will realise later that it is in your best interest.

13 Pay careful attention to your money and your belongings. There may be some loss or theft.

14 You may square off an old problem with someone and become friends again. You can do this by talking about the problem with a willingness to forgive.

15 You could be getting very tired from overwork. Additionally, relatives are also asking you to do more. You'll need to stagger your workload.

16 Your seriousness might limit professional opportunities, but those who understand you will still support you and steer you in the right direction.

17 You should not spread yourself too thinly in your attempt to do the impossible. Check your calendar and make a schedule of the time available.

18 Just because you feel that you are at an end right now doesn't mean you can't educate yourself on how to break this cycle. Learn something new.

19 You need one more piece of information to finish off a project. This requires a journey that could be inconvenient—but it will be worth the effort.

20 Although you are generally fulfilled today, you might feel some niggling dissatisfaction within you. Get busy and put this discomfort aside.

21 Sometimes, the devil you know is better than the devil you don't. You are tempted to make a change based upon boredom rather than fact.

22 Understanding your desires will give you an insight into the frustrations you are experiencing now. Pop psychology and self-help books can give you clarity today.

23 Being a respectable worker doesn't mean you'll become rich. Sometimes, ruthlessness is necessary to achieve your goals.

24 Someone may be playing a game of chicken with you to test your courage. Don't give up until you win this round, otherwise you'll be used over and over again.

25 Sometimes, an arcane methodology is superior to a modern one. You may be ridiculed for using a tried and tested approach.

26 You can resolve some long-standing issue by being open to the other person's point of view. Be compassionate in your attitude and it will work wonders.

27 If you're feeling depressed today, it is because you have too much time on your hands to think about yourself. Consider others first and you can overcome this.

28 You must conclude an incident that has been dragging on for some time now, possibly with a close relative. You may as well be the one to make the first move.

29 You seem to be duplicating work by overlooking some important details. Analyse these details first and you will save a lot of time.

30 You don't have to be trendy to be different; you need to dress to express your personality and mood. Don't be swayed by fads.

31 Improving your vocabulary is essential during this cycle if you want to make a better impression. All you need to do is learn one or two new words a day to extend your language skills.

⊚ NOVEMBER ⊚

Monthly Highlights

Your popularity will increase when Venus moves through the upper part of your horoscope. Friendships are powerful after the 5th, and you may not realise just how respected and needed you are by others. But this is a double-edged sword, especially if you are needed too much. Know where to draw the line and say no if people are expecting too much from you right now.

The Sun and Jupiter continue to bring you good fortune, and when the Sun enters your zone of professional accomplishments after the 22nd, you can look forward to an excellent cycle in your career life.

1 Considering someone's requests today need not take up too much time. You'll know immediately whether or not you should say yes or no.

2 There's no point complicating a relationship you are not keen on. But if you are afraid of speaking your mind, this is exactly what will happen. Don't beat around the bush.

3 If you are suffering some abuse, the choice is yours as to whether or not you continue taking it. You need to seek legal and/or psychological advice.

4 Once again, financial projections are necessary if you are to keep your head above water. You are getting swept away in the excitement of the moment and spending more than you should.

5 You may be dominated by your partner when it comes to spending. You need to set a strict budgetary plan.

6 You need plenty of stimulation today to inspire you to do bigger and better things. This may involve a change of environment, even if it is only temporary.

7 You're making yourself emotionally vulnerable by giving too much of yourself to others. Put aside some time for yourself.

8 Keep identification with you today as you may overlook some essential paperwork. Check your bag or wallet before you leave.

9 Diversity and broadmindedness are your keywords today. This will be necessary to keep abreast of the demands of your work and social life. You may need to discuss many topics just now.

10 There might be some discomfort dining with someone of importance right now. Simply be yourself and you'll be surprised at how much respect you get.

11 If you're not successful in your attempts to acquire a new job, remember that each session will reveal more of what is necessary to get the job. Practice makes perfect.

12 You may need to dangle a carrot to someone if you want some relief in your busy schedule. A friend may be prepared to help, but only if there's something in it for them.

13 If you give an inch, someone will take a mile, so you mustn't indulge another person's desire to take advantage of your goodwill.

14 You may experience frustration today, which is why you will need elaborate guidelines on how to conduct yourself, work equipment or deal with someone.

15 Finding the culprit today may not be easy, and your suspicion of several people may be unjustified. Don't accuse anyone before you know the truth.

16 Being in public may be uncomfortable today. You have more important and private things to do. Take a rain check on the appointment.

17 Releasing tension may simply be a matter of enjoying some soothing music or having a coffee with a friend.

18 Your moods are fluctuating at the moment, so you need to find a way to even out your temperament. Try some deep breathing, or, better still, some intense exercise.

19 You may be baffled by a problem, but your ego won't allow you to ask someone for help. So be it. Don't be surprised when it takes you a lot more time to work it out.

20 You need to crawl before you can walk, which is why you may be annoyed that you can't do something as efficiently as you would like. Enjoy the journey to perfection.

21 Reminiscing with friends is great. But it will bring up a whole lot of old memories that will rekindle feelings—some good and some bad.

22 Keeping others at arm's length give you a distinct advantage, especially if you feel you are being used. Create desire and value yourself.

23 Your vision of work is eclipsing your personal life right now. You may need to make some concessions, even though your loyalties are divided.

24 Be organised in the way that you work through your chores today. If you start too many things, you will get nothing done.

25 You may serve someone only to find that they strike back at you for no apparent reason. You must understand that they are reacting to their own personal issues.

26 Repeating yourself could make you angry, but it is the only way you'll get through to someone who is insensitive. You will be a catalyst for change in their lives.

27 If you ignore alarm bells and red flags when you meet someone, there is no one to blame but yourself.

28 You may meet someone with a rather warped intellect, but this will be a refreshing change from the humdrum individuals you've been dealing with.

29 You may want to buy big-ticket items, but you must do so in consultation with your spouse or partner. This could start a mini war.

30 Your attitude will affect a verdict today—and it is not what you were hoping for. Your desire will take a little longer to be fulfilled.

⊚ DECEMBER ⊚

Monthly Highlights

You may receive a promotion this month, probably after the 3rd. If it is not a promotion in the traditional sense, you may feel as though you have achieved something or you will receive some good feedback, which means that doors are opening for you. Increased income, a pay rise or perhaps a lump sum payout after the 22nd will be a welcome relief, especially if you had some extra bills this month. Just make sure you don't spend it all in one go. Merry Christmas!

1 You need to extend the range and diversity of your skills as you are finding that your abilities are limited at the moment. You possess greater talents than you realise.

2 You may get annoyed when someone gives you the run-around over some red tape or correspondence. Get straight to the point and don't be too diplomatic.

3 Continual interruptions will make you weary, and you may consider 'disappearing for a while' for the sake of getting the job done.

4 The people around you are unstable today, and this is cause for concern. If you are in a workplace that is lacking in discipline, you may have to consider alternative options.

5 Today you can enjoy being with others in a friendly, sociable and even flirtatious manner.

6 Talk about the future of your family with your partner and try to make some changes in your domestic life today.

7 Someone you least expected can help you unravel a problem or reduce the lack of attention you are experiencing in your life right now.

8 Someone isn't providing you with the tools required to do a job properly. You need to make your demands known, preferably in writing.

9 You could lose trust in someone when you discover that they lied to you. You may need to think about the future of your relationship with them.

10 It is never too late to fulfil a dream. If you're feeling remorse about this, you can still pick up the pieces and make another attempt.

11 You're apprehensive about replacing some of your old ways with new ones. But the moment you instigate this new course of action, you will breathe a sigh of relief.

12 If you are in a new relationship, a twist of fate may change things in a way you hadn't expected. Be prepared for major changes that will radically alter your attitude.

13 You are not happy with the way a health practitioner has handled your issue and you may be at your wit's end trying to solve this problem. Seek a second opinion.

14 Don't allow too many relatives, particularly in-laws, to gain too much information about your personal life. This can make life hell on earth.

15 You may feel that you're blindfolded at the moment and don't know which way to turn. You have a problem to solve, but you don't have the means to solve it.

16 Something of value may have disappeared and you may not be able to find it. Don't go out and buy a new one yet; it may turn up.

17 You have to entertain or handle too many people at work. You will be feeling stifled by this prospect, but there is no way of avoiding it.

18 Friends are not available to support you today. If you have been misjudged or misunderstood, talk about it to find out why they are absent in your time of need.

19 There will be an unusual offer on the table that may relate to some sort of relationship or sexual affair.

20 Someone is expecting something from you, but you are dodging them because you are running behind schedule. You need to make this a priority.

21 You may have a sticky or problematic client today, and you'll be tested on how you manage the client to achieve a win-win situation.

22 You're micromanaging a situation and forgetting the big picture. Don't get bogged down in the little things today.

23 Don't be afraid to pay more for items that will last longer than their cheaper versions. It's better to pay more for quality.

24 Don't allow anger to lurk beneath the surface. It will erode your peace of mind and your health. Call a spade a spade and address the issue with the person in question.

25 Christmas may have a deeper significance for you this year, but it can still be a fun day.

26 If things have been a bit lacklustre in the bedroom lately, it could be because work commitments have become an unwelcome distraction.

27 You could be made to feel the perfect fool only to find that it's one big joke. Try not to take things too seriously today.

28 Someone is taking your affection for granted. You need to withdraw to create greater value in yourself. This should work.

29 If you're travelling, you may find yourself confined at your destination. This may have to do with the weather, facilities or the people you are with.

30 You may prefer to spend some time alone to recover from a rather busy period. Make no apologies for this. You deserve it.

31 It's time to renew a friendship with someone today. Some deeper emotional issues are at stake.

2013
ASTRONUMEROLOGY

THE BEST THINGS IN LIFE ARE SILLY.

Scott Adams

THE POWER BEHIND
⊚ YOUR NAME ⊚

Did you know that your name actually resonates at a certain frequency, a vibration that is unique to you? To find out what this vibration is, and how it affects you and your destiny, you simply add the numbers of your name to reveal which planet is governing you. This is an ancient form of numerology based upon the Chaldean system in which each number is assigned a planetary vibration. Take a look at the chart below to see how each alphabetical letter is connected to a planetary energy.

AIJQY	=	1	Sun
BKR	=	2	Moon
CGLS	=	3	Jupiter
DMT	=	4	Uranus
EHNX	=	5	Mercury
UVW	=	6	Venus
OZ	=	7	Neptune
FP	=	8	Saturn
—	=	9	Mars

Note: The number 9 is not allotted a letter because it is a mysterious vibration and considered 'unknowable'.

Once the numbers have been added together, they result in a number which is associated with a planet that rules your name and personal affairs.

It is no accident that many famous actors, writers and musicians have modified their names. They use these name changes to attract luck and good fortune, which can be facilitated by using the energies of a friendlier planet. Try experimenting with the table and see how new names affect you. It's so much fun and may even attract greater love, wealth and worldly success!

By studying the following example, you too can work out the power of your name. If your name is Andrew Brown, calculate the ruling planet by correlating each letter to a number in the table, like this:

A	N	D	E	W		B	R	O	W	N
1	5	4	2	5	6		2	2	7	6	5

And then add the numbers like this:

$$1 + 5 + 4 + 2 + 5 + 6 + 2 + 2 + 7 + 6 + 5 \quad = \quad 45$$

Then add $\qquad 4 + 5 \quad = \quad 9$

The ruling number of Andrew Brown's name is 9, which is ruled by Mars. (See how the nine can now be used?) Now study the Name-Number Table to reveal the power of your name. The numbers 4 and 5 will play a secondary role in Andrew's character and destiny, so in this case you would also study the effects of Uranus (4) and Mercury (5).

Your Name Number	Ruling Planet	Your Name Characteristics
1	Sun	Beautiful character. Able to sway people with their charm. Physically active. They enjoy sports and other competitive activities. Many friends and rich and wealthy well-wishers. Excellent connections in government circles and with political individuals. Makes a wonderful friend. Can be loyal but stubborn.
2	Moon	Soft, receptive and emotional by nature. Extreme change of moods. Highly sensitive and psychic. Curious nature, kind-hearted and creative in many areas. Strong love of family and friends. Prefers night to day. Women have a strong karmic influence on them.

Your Name Number	Ruling Planet	Your Name Characteristics
3	Jupiter	Strong philosophical nature. Supreme optimist but at times opportunistic, which is unnecessary because a great deal of luck is associated with Jupiter. Great sense of timing. Expansive and generous nature that may be wasteful at times. Travel will bring them many interesting experiences.
4	Uranus	Unusual character with an erratic nature. Unusual likes and dislikes. Many unexpected experiences, ups and downs and interesting but short-lived relationships. May become bored easily and needs to plan more carefully for a stable life.
5	Mercury	Master communicator. A love of change and variety which may lead to an ever-shifting pattern of life without stability. Always young at heart, playful and attractive to all. Attracted to the written and spoken word. Quick witted.

Your Name Number	Ruling Planet	Your Name Characteristics
6	Venus	Seductive and delightful personality. Gracious and social by nature. Eye-catching personality with a variety of friends. Expert in bedroom arts and also able to make money through social activities. Music, art and other aesthetic activities take pride of place in life. Strong family ties that need to be carefully balanced with career appetites.
7	Neptune	One of the most spiritual numbers, which indicates a psychic and self-sacrificing nature. Unconditional in love and able to develop the most altruistic character. Prophetic, a dreamer, but sometimes victimised by the very people they wish to help. Can be a romantic idealist.

Your Name Number	Ruling Planet	Your Name Characteristics
8	Saturn	An excessively hard worker, sometimes overly preoccupied by money and security. Great powers of concentration. Will usually work long and hard to achieve ambitions. Slow in giving trust and demands perfection in all areas of life. Sometimes overly serious, but a loyal character.
9	Mars	Immense stamina and recuperative powers. Highly physical and sexual individual. Often steamrolls others, but means well. Combative, competitive, arrogant and playful. Injury-prone. Protects family and is extremely loyal to all he or she considers important. Great success through sheer effort.

YOUR PLANETARY
◎ RULER ◎

Astrology and numerology are very closely aligned. Each planet rules over a number between 1 and 9. Both your name and your birth date are ruled by planetary energies. Here are the planets and their ruling numbers:

1   **Sun**

2   **Moon**

3   **Jupiter**

4   **Uranus**

5   **Mercury**

6   **Venus**

7   **Neptune**

8   **Saturn**

9   **Mars**

To find out which planet will control the coming year for you; simply add the numbers of your birth date and the year in question. Here is an example:

If you were born on 12 November, add the numerals 1 and 2 (12, your day of birth) and 1 and 1 (11, your month of birth) to the year in question, in this case 2013 (current year), like this:

Add 1 + 2 + 1 + 1 + 2 + 0 + 1 + 3   =   **11**

                               1 + 1   =   **2**

The planet ruling your individual karma for 2013 will be the Moon because this planet rules the number 2.

YOUR PLANETARY
◎ FORECAST ◎

You can even take your ruling name number, as shown above, and add it to the year in question to throw more light on your coming personal affairs, like this:

A N D R E W B R O W N	**=**	**9**
Year coming	**=**	**2013**
Add 9 + 2 + 0 + 1 + 3	**=**	**15**
Add 1 + 5	**=**	**6**

This is the ruling year number using your name number as a basis. You would then study the influence of Venus (6) for 2013. Good luck!

Trends for Your Planetary Number in 2013

Year Number	Ruling Planet	Results Throughout the Coming Year
1	Sun	

Overview

The commencement of a new cycle: a year full of accomplishments, increased reputation, brand new plans and projects. New responsibilities, success and strong physical vitality. Health should improve and illnesses will be healed. If you have ailments, this is the time to improve your physical wellbeing—recovery will be certain.

Love and pleasure

A lucky year for love. Credit connection with children. Family life is in focus. Music, art and creative expression will be fulfilling. New romantic opportunities.

Work

Minimal effort for maximum luck. Extra money and exciting professional opportunities. Positive new changes result in promotion and pay rises.

Improving your luck

Luck is plentiful, particularly in July and August. The 1st, 8th, 15th and 22nd hours of Sundays are lucky.

Your lucky numbers are 1, 10, 19 and 28.

Year Number	Ruling Planet	Results Throughout the Coming Year
2	Moon	

Overview

Reconnection with your emotions and past. Excellent for relationships with family members. Moodiness may become a problem. Sleeping patterns will be affected.

Love and pleasure

Home, family life and relationships are in focus this year. Relationships improve through self-effort and greater communication. Change of residence, renovations and interior decoration bring satisfaction. Increased psychic sensitivity.

Work

Emotional in work. Home career, or hobby from a domestic base, will bring greater income opportunities. Females will be more prominent in your work.

Improving your luck

July will fulfil some of your dreams. Monday will be lucky with the 1st, 8th, 15th and 22nd hours being particularly fortunate. Pay special attention to the New and Full Moons in 2013.

Your lucky numbers include 2, 11, 20, 29 and 38.

Year Number	Ruling Planet	Results Throughout the Coming Year
3	Jupiter	

Overview

A lucky year for you. Exciting opportunities will expand your horizons. Good fortune financially. Travels and increased popularity. A happy year. Your spiritual inclinations will grow and you will also want to explore the world. Travel is on the cards.

Love and pleasure

You feel confident about romance during this cycle. You may meet someone during busy activity or while travelling. This is a good opportunity to deepen your love for your partner.

Work

Fortunate for new opportunities and success. Employers are more accommodating and open to your creative expression. Extra money. New job promotions are possible.

Improving your luck

Remain realistic, get more sleep and don't expect too much from your efforts. Planning is necessary for better luck. The 1st, 8th, 15th and 24th hours of Thursdays are spiritually very lucky for you.

Year Number	Ruling Planet	Results Throughout the Coming Year
3	Jupiter	Your lucky numbers are 3, 12, 21, and 30. March and December are lucky months. 2013 will bring you some unexpected surprises.

Year Number	Ruling Planet	Results Throughout the Coming Year
4	Uranus	

Overview

Don't take things for granted during this cycle as changes may occur when you least expect them. Unexpected twists and turns of fate. Possibility of having to begin all over again. Progressive attitude may bring many unusual and uplifting experiences.

Love and pleasure

Guard against dissatisfaction in relationships. You require plenty of freedom and experimentation. Love may take you by surprise. You could meet someone when you least expect it, but the relationship may turn out to be tumultuous.

Work

Unusual and modern lines of work are likely in the coming year and you need to be open to new ideas to enhance your career prospects. Working with technological apparatus, software and other online tools will be of interest to you. Try not to overwork and find ways to reduce your stress levels.

Year Number	Ruling Planet	Results Throughout the Coming Year
4	Uranus	**Improving your luck**

Temperance is your keyword in the coming 12 months. Be patient and do not rush things. Slow your pace this year as impulse will only lead to errors and missed opportunities. Exercise greater patience in all matters. Steady investments are lucky.

The 1st, 8th, 15th and 20th hours of any Saturday will be very lucky for you in 2013.

Your lucky numbers are 4, 13, 22 and 31.

Year Number	Ruling Planet	Results Throughout the Coming Year
5	Mercury	

Overview

You are moving so quickly that things appear to be in fast-forward mode. You need to pace yourself, even if your imagination and communication skills are at a peak. New ideas will fascinate you and life will seem full of opportunities.

Intellectual activities and communications increase. Your imagination is powerful. New and exciting ideas will bring success and personal satisfaction.

Love and pleasure

Relationships take on a more playful air in 2013. You must be adaptable to keep pace with your family members and your own schedule. Love affairs may be confusing as you could become indecisive. Try to accept your spouse or partner for who they are. You may become critical. Learn to curb your impulse to find fault.

Work

Your innovative ideas put you ahead of your work peers. You will meet many people and may also develop an interest in commerce and finance. You will want to trade and increase profitability in your business.

Year Number	Ruling Planet	Results Throughout the Coming Year
5	Mercury	You can achieve a senior position if you are prepared to assume additional responsibilities. Don't do too much. Speed, efficiency and capability are your keywords this year. Don't be impulsive in making a career change. Travel is also on your agenda.

Improving your luck

Write down your ideas, research topics more thoroughly, and communicate your enthusiasm through meetings. This will afford you much more luck. Stick to one idea.

The 1st, 8th, 15th and 20th hours of Wednesday are luckiest, so schedule your meetings and other important social engagements at these times.

Your lucky numbers are 5, 14, 23 and 32.

Year Number	Ruling Planet	Results Throughout the Coming Year
6	Venus	

Overview

2013 will be an important year for romance and new relationships. You will be sensual as well as sexually self-indulgent. Your family affairs will take precedence over other aspects of your life. You may want to work with the one you love. Money should be plentiful, but only if you reduce your overheads and unnecessary expenses.

Love and pleasure

Your keyword in the next 12 months is romance. An existing romance is deepened now. You may meet someone new who can help you develop greater self-esteem. You will take on a new look. Put your best foot forward. Engagement, or even marriage, is quite possible. Increase in social responsibilities. Moderate your excessive tendencies.

Work

Your protective instincts and desire for greater future security will dominate your working life. You will be finding ways to cut back costs and save more money. Combining your professional and domestic life is also likely. Working from home may be preferable.

Year Number	Ruling Planet	Results Throughout the Coming Year
6	Venus	**Improving your luck**

Work and success are dependent on your creative and positive mental attitude. Eliminate bad habits and personality tendencies that can obstruct you. Balance spiritual and financial needs.

The 1st, 8th, 15th and 20th hours on Fridays are extremely lucky for you this year and new opportunities can arise when you least expect it.

The numbers 6, 15, 24 and 33 will generally increase your luck.

Year Number	Ruling Planet	Results Throughout the Coming Year
7	Neptune	

Overview

This is an intuitive and spiritually karmic year. Your life goals become more focused, but you need to rely on your inner resources to get you across the line. You need to be careful of people who might use you this year. Don't be too trusting.

Love and pleasure

You may meet someone who is your spiritual soul mate this year. Your love is idealistic and you will not settle for anything less than perfect. You may put people on pedestals because you are not seeing their character clearly. Try to look at people truthfully.

Work

You may wish to become involved in humanitarian work or get involved in activities that can help you foster your spiritual ideals. Clearing out your environment of negative vibrations will help you focus and become more successful. Use your intuition in any job move. Your hunches will be correct.

Year Number	Ruling Planet	Results Throughout the Coming Year
7	Neptune	**Improving your luck**

Be very clear in what you are trying to communicate and stick to one path this year for best results. Pay attention to your health and don't let this stress affect your positive outlook. Sleep well, exercise and develop better eating habits to allow greater energy circulation.

The 1st, 8th, 15th and 20th hours of Wednesday are your luckiest, so schedule your meetings and other important social engagements at these times.

Your lucky numbers are 5, 14, 23 and 32.

Year Number	Ruling Planet	Results Throughout the Coming Year
8	Saturn	

Overview

You have passed previous tests in life and should now be strong enough to deal with anything that life throws at you. You need to be practical and pay attention to traditional structures, and other conservative requirements.

You could become a workaholic, so pace yourself and make sure your diary is not jam-packed. Finances should improve through your efforts.

Love and pleasure

Try not to be too serious about your relationships and keep the fun alive. Don't be too demanding and balance your professional and domestic life to keep loved ones happy. Dedicate time to your family, not just work. Schedule activities outdoors to increase your wellbeing and emotional satisfaction.

Work

Money is your focus throughout 2013, but this will require hard work on your part. You may need to make some hard decisions that could cost you friends as you choose security over outdated relationships.

Year Number	Ruling Planet	Results Throughout the Coming Year
8	**Saturn**	**Improving your luck**

Being too cautious may cause you to miss opportunities during the coming 12 months. If new opportunities are offered, balance your head and your heart when drawing conclusions. You may be reluctant to attempt something new. Be kind to yourself and don't overwork or overdo exercise.

The 1st, 8th, 15th and 20th hours of Saturdays are the best times for you in 2013.

Your lucky numbers are 1, 8, 17, 26 and 35.

Year Number	Ruling Planet	Results Throughout the Coming Year
9	Mars	

Overview

In a 9 year, you will see old chapters closing and new ones opening. This may not be an easy cycle as you transition to bigger and better things. Remain open and don't hold onto the past. Do not be impulsive or irritable. Avoid arguments. Calm communication will help find solutions.

Love and pleasure

You have strong sexual impulses during this cycle. You will enjoy your sexual intimacy. Romance is dependent on personal wellbeing, so do loads of exercise to keep fit. Receptive understanding of your lovers will bring about a new and improved state of affairs. Listen carefully to your partner's needs and try to fulfil them.

Work

This is the year when your drive and industry will provide you with excellent results. There are bigger and better things on the horizon and you will actively make them happen. You are likely to take on a leadership role and receive respect and honour from others—as long as you are fair in your dealings with them.

Year Number	Ruling Planet	Results Throughout the Coming Year
9	Mars	**Improving your luck**

Find an outlet for your high level of energy through meditation, self-reflection and prayer. Collect your energies and focus them on one point. Release tension to maintain health.

The 1st, 8th, 15th and 20th hours of Tuesday will be lucky for you throughout 2013.

Your lucky numbers are 9, 18, 27 and 36.